Consumers' Guide to the Protection of the Environment

It is a fact of life that the goods we buy, and the services we use, affect the environment in which we live. Each penny paid for the process that pollutes and the food that does not nourish, prolongs and expands the squandering of our resources and the pollution of the environment on which we ultimately depend.

The Consumers' Guide is essentially an action guide for the individual – and especially for the housewife. It tells exactly how we can direct our consumer habits so that we can relate our way of life to the ability of the environment to support our real needs.

Jonathan Holliman, aged 25, studied geography and botany at University College, London. He has been actively involved in environmental issues both here and abroad for more than ten years. Working mostly with youth groups, he has concentrated on environmental education and is a member of the Education Commission of the International Union for Conservation of Nature and Natural Resources. Presently director of the International Youth Centre for Environmental Affairs and a spare-time director of Friends of the Earth Ltd, this is his first book, but has contributed to others including *The Environmental Handbook – Action Guide for the UK* published by Pan/Ballantine.

Consumers' Guide to the Protection of the Environment

JONATHAN HOLLIMAN

This book was based on the American book, *The User's Guide to the Protection of the Environment* by Paul Swatek for Friends of the Earth in the United States of America.

A PAN/BALLANTINE BOOK
published in association with
FRIENDS OF THE EARTH

First published in Great Britain in 1971
This book is published jointly by Ballantine Books Ltd,
and Pan Books Ltd
of 33 Tothill Street, London S.W.1

ISBN 345 09701 7

Printed in Great Britain by
Cox and Wyman Ltd, London, Reading and
Fakenham

To the tree from which this book was made

CONTENTS

1. INTRODUCTION

1 INTRODUCTION

HOW DOES THE CONSUMER FIT IN?

Every consumer decision we make has an impact on the environment. This is an ecological fact of life. Every time we go shopping, use public or private transport, or choose a place to live in, our choices have an effect, for better or worse, on the quality of the air we breathe and the water we drink – on the world we experience with our eyes and ears and noses.

It is not always easy to see the connexions, but we are getting better at recognizing them. Clearly, the paper we buy as packaging and then throw away was once a tree, and the electric power that flows from the wall sockets comes from a fossil fuel plant, nuclear reactor, or hydro-electric dam. We should also recognize that motor car owners must also share a part of the blame for oil tanker disasters such as the *Torrey Canyon*.

But we really *need* many things which ultimately influence our environment – we need shelter, food, leisure, and a generally satisfying standard of living. However, there are many things we do *not* need. At present our whole society is based on a vicious circle of ever-increasing production and consumption, without questioning whether we are really any healthier or happier for it. By seductive and clever advertising and salesmanship we are constantly brainwashed to consume what the manufacturer wants us to, and not what we really need.

Certainly the state of the environment is the clearest indication that some of our cherished values may be wrong.

As the population has grown and as the consumption rate of each individual has increased, living in an industrial society like Britain has also meant traffic jams, foul air, crowded cities (and coasts), deteriorating public services, and mounting levels of noise, solid wastes, and pesticide residues. Achieving a high degree of freedom from material want has also meant a crescendo of environmental problems that in the long-term threaten the supply of food and raw materials for everyone.

It is certainly not easy for the individual to do much about these more far-reaching effects of our inflated consumption rate. What people *can* control, however, is the extent to which their individual actions contribute to these major collective problems. This is important because up to now it is the escalation of individual *consumption*, more than the increase in our numbers, that has so adversely affected the quality of our environment.

The challenge to the concerned consumer will be to use his buying power to vote against the behaviour that has brought us to the present situation. He must be acutely aware that each penny paid for the product that is harmful or unnecessary, the process that pollutes, or the food that doesn't nourish, prolongs and expands the squandering of our resources and destroys the biological systems on which we ultimately depend.

YOUR BEST GUIDE IS COMMON SENSE

One of the problems of giving advice about the environmental effects of various products is the difficulty of being definite about what is ecologically good and what is ecologically bad. Ecologists tend to be cautious people without instant solutions. Unfortunately, their long-term perspectives tend to get overridden by short-term political and economic pressures. And in response to the bewildering array of environmental problems and crises we are offered an equally bewildering array of 'solutions', some valid, others not.

The issues are complex and sometimes overwhelming – but it is practical, immediate advice consumers need, and that is what this book seeks to provide.

In many cases it is extremely difficult to get 'the facts', and even harder to verify them. This is true not just for the concerned consumer, but even for the compiler of a consumers' guide, because industries and government departments maintain a policy of secrecy that leaves communication of information up to public relations men and politicians. These people too often have neither the technical background nor, unfortunately, the freedom from financial interest to enable them to communicate information accurately.

Another problem is that 'the facts' are constantly changing. This is especially true of product formulae such as detergents, and unless there is a simple way for the consumer to learn the ingredients of what he is buying – from the label, for example – he cannot make an informed choice without special inquiries. He may also still have to make special inquiries about some of the products listed in this book, as the book, of course, cannot change with time.

Perhaps the best guide to making consumer decisions count is common sense. As we increase our knowledge of environmental issues, the more we realize how many unanswered questions there are. It is therefore important to understand the underlying reasons given for the specific ideas in this book so that you can develop your own ideas for action and spot new dangers as they come along.

It is also obvious that many of the ideas may take extra time and trouble. It is easy to give in to the feeling that 'my own contribution won't make much difference', but this must be resisted. Experiment for yourself; take a normal day and measure the amount of electricity you use, then practise some of the ideas that follow for a week and see the difference – now multiply that difference 56 million times and you'll see what a national effort could do. You are also sure to find that some things will be cheaper, more pleasant and easier than you think.

At a personal level the following pages seek to demonstrate that there is an alternative to the consumptive rat race. This book attempts to look beyond material needs to values which cannot be measured only in terms of growth in the Gross National Product. In rational, palatable steps, you, the consumer, can modify your daily habits to bring them more into balance with your environment. The benefits to the individual may surprise you – for mankind it could mean survival.

GENERAL CONSIDERATIONS

Some environmental terms

Before going any farther, let's take a look at a few words. Some of them may be new; familiar ones may be viewed in a new light.

Biodegradability. Man has created a large number of substances which were not previously found in the natural world, and he produces others in such quantities as never occurred before. Those which break down rapidly on their own, or through the action of organisms, are termed biodegradable. Others are so unnatural that the organisms which live on this planet have no way of chewing them up. Such long-lasting, non-biodegradable products as DDT, and plastics present problems when they interact adversely with living things, or accumulate to the point that they take up too much space.

Ecology. Ecology has been around for a long time as a science, a science that has examined the ways in which plants and animals relate to each other and to their physical environments. However, it is no longer possible to view ecology as being concerned only with Venus' fly-traps and flies, or with frogs and lily pads, because suddenly man has discovered that he, too, is a part of the ecological system.

Ecosystems. Living things that relate to each other as predators, or by sharing food or living space, are said to be part of an ecosystem. In stable ecosystems, interrelationships among the different members work out so that each mutually supports the continued existence of the other members, as well as the continuity of the system itself. A woodland meadow, a puddle of rainwater, and our own digestive tracts, are all ecosystems. The ultimate ecosystem man is likely to deal with is the solar system.

Ecological Cycles. Natural systems tend to order themselves so that the wastes of one member are the food for another. In this way the resources of the system are conserved. Thus, plants turn carbon dioxide into oxygen which, in turn, gets used by animals to burn up their food, a process which regenerates the carbon dioxide.

Energy. When we consider the planet Earth as man's ecosystem, energy turns out to be the one renewable resource. Ultimately this energy comes from the sun. The life-support system that has evolved on this planet, with its cycles and interdependent ecosystems, provides the mechanisms by which the energy in sunlight gets trapped (by photosynthesis) and distributed throughout the system. Man needs this energy to make his muscles move, to generate heat to keep him warm and to cook his food, to transport him from place to place, and to run his industries. Because energy is the ultimate resource, other resources are often measured in terms of it.

Environment. Generally speaking, environment is everything – physical and otherwise – that surrounds us. It falls into two main parts: the socio-cultural environment which is man-oriented and includes our social systems, family units and behaviour relations to each other, and the biophysical which includes all other living things and the natural elements such as water, air, minerals, etc. Both interrelate to form the total environment which surrounds every living thing.

Eutrophication. This is an ageing process which normally happens very slowly, on a time scale of many tens of thousands of years. But since the appearance of technological man, the process has been accelerated enormously. An estimate has been made that Lake Erie – a large lake in the USA that has been the recipient of tons of industrial waste – has aged 15,000 years since 1920! Eutrophication begins when there is an excess of all the nutrients that algae

U.S. FEARS OF
FUEL CRISIS
RECEDE

By Our Washington Staff

America's petrol shortage may not be as acute this summer as was originally feared. Refinery production is up and fuel consumption is growing more slowly than was forecast.

Many petrol stations are getting increased petrol quotas from suppliers and relaxing their restrictions on opening hours and fuel sales.

Meanwhile, Pan American Airways says it will reduce flight speeds to cut consumption of fuel by more than 10 million gallons in the next year. Cruising speeds on cargo and passenger flights will drop from 542 mph to 529 mph.

Grable. James
Made Me Love
d to uncover a
ynn, a widower
fe in love with
mmer (B B C-1,
lack Mountains
re.

Desk. **7,** News;
core. **7.30,** Sports
73 (series) (S).
Up Country (S).
2 Ballroom
). **10,** News; Late
a (**10.15,** Sports
News) (**VHF,** As
12, News. **12.5,**
(S) (**1,** News).

4, 188m & VHF)

s, Weather; Your
Choice, recds (S)
9, News: This
omposer (S) —
9.45, Ibert recdg
The Lighter
11, Music for
11.35, Words . . .
City of Glasgow
Junior Violin

---

from **OUTSIDE**

OPERA AND
• **MATINEE**

COLISEUM.
Until July 1
CHINESE AC
THEATRE OF
70 of the world's

COVENT GARDEN.
OPERA. Tonight a
Opera House Benevo
Tomorrow & Mon.
last perf. R

IL BARBE
DI SIVIG
Sat. & Tues. next
CARMEN. Seats and
Mon. next. (240 10

COVENT GARDEN.
BALLET. Fri. &
7.30: SCENES
ENIGMA VARIAT
& CHLOE. Sat. &
School in MORE
SOLITAIRE, THE
available Sat, &
few for Fri.,
only. (240 1066).

GLYNDEBOURNE FE
Until Aug. 15 w
Philharmonic Orc
Fri. at 5.30. Sun
verdi's "Il ritorn
patria," tomorro
5.10 Mozart's
Figaro," possible
at short notice
Glyndebourne.
812411) and Ibl
Wigmore,

and aquatic plants need to grow. The plants then grow to excess, die, and rot. This process is repeated until the lake becomes a bog, and eventually, dry land. Phosphorus, from detergents and other forms of municipal waste, is a big factor in accelerating the eutrophication process.

Interdependence. The various ecosystems are themselves interdependent – if one is disturbed, adjustments may be required in others that seem far removed.

Non-renewable Resources. Man lives on a planet with finite resources. That is to say, he has so much land and clean water, so much oxygen, so much tin, and no more. The planet contains large, but not unlimited, quantities of coal and oil (the so-called fossil fuels) and high-grade mineral ores.

Pollution. In a broad sense, pollution is anything that interferes with the proper functioning of the ecosystem. It can include many naturally occurring materials as well as such unnatural substances as DDT and nuclear fall-out. Phosphates and nitrates, essential in *low* concentrations as nutrients, pollute lakes and rivers in the high concentrations that sewage treatment plants and agricultural run-off produce. Water released from a cooling tower as a fog must also be considered a pollutant. Noise pollution, sustained at more than 80 decibels, can cause physiological as well as psychological effects.

Recycling. When natural mechanisms for bringing one of man's waste products back into an ecological cycle do not exist, man must devise a way of recycling it – or ultimately forgo further use of that resource. Man chops down trees to make fibre, out of which he makes paper. Unless used paper is repulped and made into new paper, more trees have to be cut down. By recovering scrap metal from junk piles man can reduce the amount of ore he takes out of the Earth. Some materials such as plastics, can be recycled only by burning them.

Stability. In spaceships, man builds back-up systems to guard against mishaps. Nature, too, adds complexity to her life-support systems to obtain adaptability and stability.

Simplifying an ecosystem, as man does in mass-production agriculture, for instance, makes the system more vulnerable – in this case to pest invastion.

Some ecological principles

There are a few ecological facts of life which should be kept in mind as you read this book and try to apply its ideas.

Everything comes from somewhere and everything ends up somewhere. While this may hardly come as a shock, neither has it served many of us as a guiding principle. Modern man's failure to keep it in mind is a cause of many of our problems.

Some of the animal behaviourists trace this human fault back to the apes, who live in trees and can let their excrement and litter drop into the void below. Compare their behaviour to that of the contemporary litterbug. Even the responsible citizen flushes most of his waste down a toilet or drain, or throws it into a rubbish bin that gets emptied by the refuse disposal department. Out of sight, out of mind.

The problem is especially severe with the urban dweller, for he is even more remote from his sources of supply than he is from the sewers that absorb his waste. Water flows in apparently unlimited quantities out of a tap; food comes prepared and packaged from the local supermarket. He never has to worry about the three pounds of cow manure that gets produced out on the farm for every two pints of milk he brings home. Once he had to haul coal and hoard his supply of lamp oil. Now his energy supply flows silently into the home through pipes and wires. Beyond a monthly or quarterly bill, the consumer has little incentive to conserve. Thus, it is small wonder that there is a severe waste problem that is threatening our land and water resources.

All systems and problems are ultimately if not intimately interrelated. It is important that this principle be kept in mind, because steps that are taken to solve one problem tend to have consequences that spill over into other areas. Technology, which has been successful largely through the technique of focusing attention on limited problems, has a distressing tendency to ignore this principle.

To be valid, technical solutions to environmental problems must be based on an appreciation of the complexity of the relevant ecosystems and must attack the root causes, not the symptoms. To illustrate, man dumps most of his sewage into watercourses at the same time that he is mining minerals and fixing nitrogen from the air to replenish the soil. If instead, this so-called 'waste' were returned to the soil as the fertilizer that it is, the poisoning of our waters with artificial fertilizer run-off, and their subsequent eutrophication could be both alleviated.

The motor car offers a dramatic illustration of this interrelatedness. Consider the major polluting industries involved. Petroleum, steel, mining, rubber, textiles, cement, and plastics are all clearly related to the car. Consider also air pollution, congestion of the courts with liability claims, urban noise, and traffic jams, and highways that destroy urban character and countryside. Striking a blow at this monster obviously will have wide-ranging effects.

In similar ways one sees that the open space, food, population, and pollution crises are inextricably tied up with urban decay, poverty, crime, and war. It doesn't make sense to squabble over which crisis is most urgent; we cannot afford the luxury of solving problems one by one. That is both obsolete and ecologically unsound anyway.

We live on a planet whose resources are finite. During the past few centuries it appeared that the resources of the land, water, and minerals were inexhaustible. This was encouraged by the prevailing Judeo-Christian ethic, and it was not until Malthus that people really began to question it. Air and water were common property and could be treated as the individual wished. More recently we have seen that even the capacity of the air and water has its limits when it comes to absorbing all of the by-products of man's high standard of living.

Most of us still place faith, however, in the infiniteness of the Earth's resources. The ocean, we believe, will continue to absorb all of the sewage we pump into it and, at the same time provide new sources of enormous quantities of food. The fact is, we have badly overharvested many of the commercially important ocean fish and the Atlantic Salmon is near extinction. The ecologically important marshes and wetlands have been so drastically reduced by 'reclamation' and 'development' that populations of fish are decreasing. And scientists continue to worry about the long-term effects of excess heat and carbon dioxide on the world climate.

Nature has spent literally millions of years refining a stable ecosystem. Her systems are complex and, precisely because of their complexity, they are able to absorb a great many of man's insults.

The most sophisticated computer models that men have devised can only roughly simulate the complex interactions and feedback networks of nature's simplest systems, let alone the ecology of a river under pollution stress. The scientific method isolates and focuses the attention on subsystems. It thus tends to generate over-simplified solutions, and also leads man to try to simplify his environment so that he can better 'control' it. In so doing, he makes the environment more vulnerable to the natural stresses and human miscalculations that are bound to occur.

Based on its recent track record, it would probably be wise to rein in technology until the technologists gain a better understanding of how their systems are interacting with natural systems. There is a vast inner frontier behind the leading edge of modern technology that begs for exploration. It is more likely that many of the practices man has developed to control the environment for his betterment have alternatives which are more ecologically sound. Biological control of insect pests offers an alternative to chemical control, to give one example. More often than not it makes sense to work with nature.

If the decision is made, instead, to forge ahead, blindly assaulting the natural life-support systems as we have been doing, we can expect only disaster. Nature fights back, and her weapons are floods, pest invasions, famine, and conflict.

Variety isn't just the spice of life; it's the essence of survival. If man is to survive he needs a rich and varied environment not only to supply his clothes, shelter, and food, but his psychological and social needs as well.

Consider man's efforts in supplying food. Many of our food plants and animals such as wheat and cows have been around for thousands of years, but all our 'domesticated' plants or animals (called cultigens) were derived originally from wild species. The original wild relatives are in many cases unknown or have disappeared but the relation of pigs to wild boars and of farm strawberries to their wild relatives are close and obvious enough. In some cases the wild animal is cropped without being domesticated (as in fishing) but most of the time man is trying to find new and improved sources of food. Each plant or animal has stored in its biological inheritance a variety of characteristics suited to different conditions. Man chooses the best or most suitable characteristics and mixes them together in exactly the same way as a prize bull is allowed to mate with cows to produce the best calves for better meat or higher milk yields.

As new areas of the world are cultivated, as old crops become afflicted by new diseases, and as higher yields are demanded, man is constantly looking for plants with new characteristics. Each time he has to dip into the 'gene pool' and pick out new combinations to produce new varieties to fit the new situations. But just as more people keep pushing for more crops to feed yet more people, then wildlife and thus our store of new genes and new foods becomes more and more limited.

This is the real danger. The vicious circle of our spiralling consumption rate means that we demand new, better and more goods, creating more pollution and degradation, which in turn reduces the variety and the capacity of the planet to supply our ever increasing needs. If we continue assaulting the natural life-support system as we have been doing we can only expect disaster.

Our civilization has moved into a new era in which certain traditional freedoms and privileges – unfettered private ownership, unlimited family size, total mobility in high-powered cars – collide head on with the ecological facts of life. There isn't any choice in the matter. Either men voluntarily control themselves, have their governments impose controls, or nature will do it with ecological catastrophe.

2. OVER-CONSUMPTION

Litter

Christmas

2 OVER-CONSUMPTION

It is not just the number of people that make ever-increasing demands on the environment, but the excessive and rapid rise in their consumption of goods and services, that contributes the greater danger at present.

This chapter is concerned with the environmental problems created by the intensive pressure to consume more and more goods. This pressure is created and maintained by an advertising and promotions industry. Its foundation is an economic system that produces goods designed to break down after a short period of time, and which generates dissatisfaction among consumers so that they repeatedly buy new versions of the same product and throw away the old one, even before its usefulness has ended.

HOW TO CONSUME WITHOUT REALLY TRYING

The control and acceleration of consumer spending is based on the constant fear of manufacturers that the market will become saturated – that is that if someone buys their 'durable' product they might not need another one for ten or twenty years. This is no good for the manufacturer who obviously wants to go on selling more and more of his product. In order to do this, he makes sure it either breaks down quickly or in some other way is made to become 'obsolete'. The manufacturer builds this obsolescence into the product and plans for it by manipulating the market, or by purposefully producing an inferior product. The manufacturer justifies this 'planned obsolescence', as it is called, by saying it is necessary for economic growth and full employment or that it is what the consumer wants.

In his fascinating book *The Wastemakers*, Vance Packard describes this process in detail and explains the three main ways in which planned obsolescence forces and manipulates consumers into buying more and more without the consumer having much real choice in the matter, especially where durability or design is concerned.

Types of obsolescence:

Obsolescence of function is created by the development of improved design or function. Obviously the modern turntable is an improvement over the old hand-wound gramophone and this type of obsolescence by mechanical improvement is usually in the consumer's interest. The improvement may also be in use of better materials or design improvement for easier use or maintenance. On the whole, when obsolescence is created by functional improvements it is to be welcomed, as it tends to make goods more efficient, last longer, or use less material – all important for rational use of resources. However, many changes, although hailed as technical improvements, may be only minor adjustments, putting right a previous bad design. This is especially the case where rapid model changes occur, such as in motor cars.

Obsolescence of quality means that the product is made so that after a certain amount of time, usually too soon from the consumer's point of view, it breaks down, collapses or wears out. Thus the manufacturer plans the product to last just as long as he thinks the consumer will find acceptable, and no longer. If it breaks down too soon obviously he will be flooded with returned items. But the length of time the consumer thinks the product *should* last can be controlled by making the product appear undesirable even before its planned time for breaking down.

Obsolescence of desirability. Since shoddy goods which break down quickly were not enough to create the high consumption rate the manufacturers wanted, other ways had to be found to increase consumption. This has been done by stimulating among consumers, a *craving* for the latest model or the newest colour or superfluous 'improvements'. The consumer cannot be satisfied with a hand-operated can-opener, for example; he must have an electric one, which consumes power (keeping the electricity suppliers happy), which has more parts likely to break down, which uses more material and costs considerably more. For some manufacturers even frequent model changes are not enough and, with envious eyes they study women's fashion – the ultimate in planned obsolescence of desirability.

The introduction of really durable goods is suppressed in several other ways:

Control of the market

The nagging fear for every manufacturer who has a large share of the market for a particular item, is that someone will come along and make a version of his product that will actually last a long time. This does not usually happen, though, since most consumer markets are so manipulated, price agreements are so devised, retail outlets so contrived, and monopolistic practices so pervasive, that someone with a superior product hasn't much chance of introducing it.

Occasionally, however, a break-through in a highly monopolized market does occur. This happened with Wilkinson Sword's introduction of the long-lasting Sword Edge razor blade. Wilkinson promoted this new razor blade for all they were worth and eventually Gillette, who practically controlled the razor blade market with their short-lived blades, had to give in.

Sometimes the consumer has been so brainwashed that a new product is not accepted even though it may have certain advantages. The Monopolies Commission forced the manufacturers to bring out a detergent which gave the housewife the choice of buying a cheaper product which had less promotional and packaging costs added to the price. This product, 'Square Deal' Surf, contains more detergent than other brands at a lower price. It is just as effective yet the housewife does not buy as much of it as its price advantages would suggest.

Control of patents

There are a number of frustrated inventors and researchers who thought that by taking their ideas to the would-be 'ideal' manufacturer their product would stand a good chance of reaching the market. However, even if the patent is bought by a manufacturer, the original idea often never reaches the marketing stage for fear of competition with inferior products already making a good profit.

Selective promotion

Some long-lasting items may be available in one sector of the market but not in others. This is controlled by advertising and distribution which promote short-lived goods for the ordinary consumer, and long-lived goods for other sectors such as industry, public utilities and the Army. The light-bulb is a good example. London Transport, for instance, would incur heavy labour costs for maintenance and replacement if the light-bulbs used in their vehicles only lasted as long as those available to the normal home consumer. So long-lasting bulbs are mass-produced for industrial use. Their long-lasting virtues are emphasized, and availability is suppressed for the household consumer market. Even though long-life bulbs give off slightly less light for the same amount of electricity they are quite acceptable for most home purposes. Also since supplies of tungsten are limited, and since more of the rare gases such as argon and neon are used for short-life bulbs, this sort of practice constitutes a waste of natural resources.

YOUR STRATEGY TO REDUCE
CONSUMPTION

Luckily for Britain, durability and reliability in products is still considered a virtue. You occasionally hear of people who take pride in their 30-year-old vacuum cleaner or radio, and so they should, for there is just no sound reason why things should not last. The benefits of technological advances and new materials in terms of durability, strength, and other qualities will never benefit the consumer, however, until he really uses his buying power to reverse the trend towards obsolescence. At the moment the consumer, the laws and organizations which are meant to protect his interests, are extremely weak. Meanwhile the growing trend towards over-consumption, disposability, etc, is having profound consequences on the quality of our environment and natural resources.

There are still several areas of over-consumption, though, where you can still have immediate influence.

FASHION

If one were to carry the ecological arguments to their logical extreme, we would all be wearing uniforms, durably constructed from the least-polluting and most readily washable material. Clearly this is not reasonable. But if you carry clothing design to the other extreme, you have the fashion industry. Buying a wardrobe that becomes obsolete in a year is clearly not very reasonable either.

There are signs that fashion changes are becoming so rapid that they become kaleidoscopic blurs. One advantage of this might be that by carrying fashion too far, people will not notice the change so much and will therefore wear what they think suits them. This is probably what is happening with skirt lengths for instance. They have been jumping up and down but more and more women seem less worried about length than they used to be.

Resist the 'advice' of the 'experts' who are making women, and men too, slaves to the dictates of the fashion industry which, of course, employs them. Instead, buy clothes that make you look attractive.

DISPOSABILITY

Disposability is another gimmick to get us to consume more. Disposable items obviously have their value where health or convenience is a vital factor but disposability is rapidly developing into a fetish. Manufacturers already provide us with disposable clothes, cutlery, etc, and promise almost anything disposable, from a chair to a complete house.

Along with planned obsolescence, disposability constitutes a waste of resources and is of questionable value to the consumer, yet the mad rush to an all-disposable world is nearer than you think. You only have to visit a hospital to see where we are heading. There, heavy use of disposables generates 10 to 15 pounds of rubbish per day per average patient. Plastics, polyvinyl chloride, and metal syringes create special complications above and beyond the problem of sheer volume.

But we don't have to live in this wasteful way. You can reduce your production of rubbish in many ways.

Cut down on your use of disposable items:

■ Use cloth napkins, handtowels, handkerchiefs, and nappies instead of throw-away paper ones. Paper panties should only be used where convenience is essential. They cost about a quarter of cheap nylon ones anyway.

■ Don't use paper towels to mop up a spill when you could do the job just as well with a sponge.

■ In the home, use only durable crockery, utensils, and glassware. There is no need to eat regularly off disposable plates; furthermore, it is expensive to do so.

■ For picnics and receptions, disposables have become

standard. Throw a party without them; show yourself that it can be done.

■ Should you decide that paper and plastics are unavoidable, at least choose the lesser of the evils. Non-coated paper decomposes and burns more readily than plastic-coated paper or plastics. If you wash and re-use them, the more durable plastic glasses might be worthy of an exception to the no-plastics rule.

■ Use paper straws instead of plastic ones, or don't use straws at all.

■ Buy screws, tacks, bolts, rubbers, etc, in boxes or loose, not mounted on thick cardboard that is then encased in plastic. Although the package may be designed largely to reduce shoplifting and for display purposes, the items are usually so cheap and the packaging so excessive that they should be avoided.

■ Buy single-ply, non-coloured toilet paper. Two-ply means double the trees used, and the dyes in coloured papers pollute the water unnecessarily.

■ Boycott products that are over-packaged – such as individually wrapped slices of cheese, sweets, and servings of food that are then enclosed in a plastic bag or a box.

■ Buy in bulk to reduce the proportion of packaging to contents.

■ Fancy packaging is meant to stimulate your buying. If you care about your environment, fancy packaging should have the opposite effect.

■ Share a magazine subscription with a friend and donate your used copies to a hospital or another institution that can use them. Terminate subscriptions to those publications that you never get around to reading. Read magazines in the library.

■ Do something to stop unsolicited mail. Ask that your name be taken off unwanted mailing lists. As a last defence, tie a postage paid business card to a brick and post it – they will be obliged to pay for the postage.

■ Buy quality. In the long run you will save money and

reduce the amount of obsolete rubbish you have to toss out.

▪ Don't discard anything that can be fixed. Either fix it yourself, take it to be repaired, or donate it to someone who can have it fixed.

Disposable clothing

Part of the reason why clothing doesn't cause much pollution is because it is basically a durable good. We buy it to last for a period of many months or years and so it doesn't involve the over-use of many resources in its production.

The introduction of disposable clothing could change all of this. Disposable nappies seem to be taking over a significant portion of the market, and the disposable bikini is about to be introduced. Paper dresses are already a reality. These are developments that should be resisted strongly on purely environmental grounds. Don't follow along. The costs to the environment of having to produce a largely disposable wardrobe and then to dispose of it are simply too great.

▪ Instead, try to make your clothes last. Buy clothes that will wear well. Alter your clothing instead of discarding it.

▪ Don't throw away clothing that someone else could use. Pass it on to a friend or a relative, or donate it to someone or some institution that deals in used clothing.

▪ Learn how to make your own clothing. Not only will it save you money, it can be fun to put your creative abilities to work.

PACKAGING

One of the worst offenders for creating unnecessary consumption and thoughtless waste of resources is the packaging industry. Not only is its production excessive but more than 90 per cent quickly ends up in the rubbish bin and is a significant, growing contribution to the quantity of waste and the cost of having to deal with it.

You pay for packaging

Most packaging is unnecessary beyond the minimum required for health, safety and the reduction of damage to contents. The cost of reasonable packaging is obviously an advantage to both manufacturer and consumer, and the consumer is probably willing to pay the price.

However, are you aware of the how much of the price is packaging and how much is the product? According to a survey by the trade magazine, *Modern Packaging*, an average of 18 per cent of the retail price went into packaging costs. The percentage varied with the type of product and the type of container. Here are some of the results.

Table 1. Percentage cost of packaging

Paint in an aerosol can	16%
Paint in a conventional metal can	5%
Toy in a film-overwrapped carton	14%
Toy mounted on a card, then sealed in plastic	8%
Motor oil in a metal can	26%
Small appliance in a corrugated carton	6%
Beer in a tinplate can	43%

Beer in a non-returnable glass bottle	36%
Frozen fish in a carton	5%
Moist pet food in a metal can	17%
Cereal in a folding carton	15%
Baby food in a glass jar	36%
Baby juice in a metal can	33%

Source: *Modern Packaging*, May 1967.

As you can see, 43 per cent of the cost of a can of beer goes directly into the dustbin – and you also pay to have it disposed of by the local council. This is wasteful, especially when there are readily available alternatives.

In general, any re-usable container will be less expensive, as long as it is re-used. Also, a large container will be proportionately less expensive because there is less packaging per product.

It is interesting to note some of the factors that allow wide differences in packaging costs to co-exist. Metal beverage cans, for example, have an advantage over the less expensive glass bottles because they can be filled more rapidly in the bottling plant. They are fast catching up with glass in beer and soft drink sales.

It is very clear that considerations other than cost determine what packaging is used. One of the key factors in the rise of packaging has been the advent of the self-service store. *The packaging now has to sell the product.* The medium has become the message. This is most clearly seen in the bubble-pack (large piece of cardboard, tiny trinket, all encased in plastic) that is so commonly used to sell novelty items or small items of stationery.

Convenience also sells products and their packages. Throw-away bottles and cans, dinners that cook in their foil packages, and twist-off caps on beverage bottles all provide convenience in their use, if not in their disposal.

Composite packaging innovations – which combine different types of material – have made packaging more versatile in meeting some of the marketing challenges mentioned above. Laminated plastic-paper-foil containers, plastic-coated paper milk cartons, cellulose windows in paper boxes, metal caps with plastic bottles, and many others illustrate what has become a major trend in packaging.

Only rarely have environmental and disposal considerations figured into the equations at all. This is obvious, when one considers where the trends are taking us.

■ Greater amounts of packaging mean that more paper, plastics, and metals must be manufactured.

■ More packaging means more solid waste.

■ The increase in the use of disposable containers increases the waste burden.

The move towards more composite packaging materials makes recycling increasingly difficult. Obviously, it is already difficult to separate metal rings from the necks of plastic bottles, and it's impossible to remove the laminated plastic portion of a paper container, thus preventing the paper from being pulped and made into another product.

The following Table summarizes some of the things you should take in to consideration when you evaluate a product in the market.

Table 2. Desirability and undesirability of packaging

Kind of Packaging	Item	Rating
No packaging or natural packaging	Some fruits	The best possible.
Returnable glass containers	Soft drinks and beer Milk	Good as long as the containers are actually returnable.
Re-usable containers	Biscuit tins Cigar boxes Steel drums	Good as long as the containers are actually used.
Non-coated paper	Bags for sweets Wrapping paper	Eventually disintegrates. Readily composts. Litter is a problem.
Non-coated cardboard	Boxes	Has more fibre than paper. This is the only area where significant recycling now takes place.
All-the-same-metal cans Steel	Regular cans	Can be recycled.

Table 2 contd.

Kind of Packaging	Item	Rating
Aluminium	Beverage cans	As litter steel will eventually rust. Aluminium is forever.
Steel cans with aluminium tops	'Pull-top' cans	The steel can be recycled the aluminium is lost.
Glass bottles with twist-off tops	Soft drinks	The metal rings around the top reduces the value of the cullet.
Wax paper	Box liners, cakes, etc.	If it's really wax, it will eventually deteriorate.
Standard 'tin' cans	Tinned fruits and vegetables	The tin (coated) and lead (solder) contaminants render these useless for recycling. (No detinning plants are active today.) As litter, they eventually rust.
Cellophane, plastics (NOT PVC, see below)	Windows in paper boxes Plastic bags	Won't degrade. Resists composting, but will burn.
Plastic-coated paper	Paper milk cartons	The plastic coating prevents the paper from decomposing.
Plastic from expanded polystyrene	Packing	Adds bulk to plastic's non-degradability.
Polyvinylchloride plastics (PVC)	Clear plastic bottles Stretch plastic wraps for meat and fish	Non-degradable. When burned, generates hydrochloric acid gas which corrodes any metal around (eg. in the incinerator).
Aluminium, foil-plastic containers	Orange juice, and yoghurt pots. Foil-lined boxes and bags	Non-degradable. The foil is not burnable.
Aluminium foil	By the roll for home uses	Lasts forever. Can't be recycled but can be re-used if careful. Resists separation in segregation systems.
Collapsible metal tubes.	Toothpaste	Not re-usable, recyclable or combustible.

Table 2 contd.

Kind of Packaging	Item	Rating
Aerosol cans	Toiletries Deodorants Hairsprays Spray paints	Enormous amount of packaging per unit net weight. Not re-usable or re-cyclable. A hazard (explosion), even when empty.

Also

■ Any aluminium product is expensive in terms of environmental costs. It takes about 10 kilowatt-hours of electricity just to make a pound of it.

■ 'Degradable' plastics have been heralded, but they have not come on the market yet. It remains to be seen whether they really do break down into harmless products.

■ Twine is preferable to rubber bands.

■ Anything that is readily discardable is potential litter.

What can you do about excess packaging?

■ Politely decline to have your purchase put in a bag whenever it isn't necessary, and explain why. Convert sales assistants.

■ Whenever a product is available in a returnable or re-usable container, buy it in that form. Milk and other beverages are still sold in returnable bottles. Look for them.

■ Be sure you return all returnable bottles.

■ To make a point, return all *non*-returnable bottles and cans to the store or manufacturer as well.

■ Leave any unnecessary overwrap at the shop before you go home. Explain to the shop manager why his toothpaste tubes or pots of cosmetics don't need a box as well.

■ Judge a product, in part, by the container it comes in. Boycott products sold only in unacceptable containers. Don't buy cheese slices individually wrapped in plastics.

■ Don't buy products in aerosol cans.

■ Don't buy TV dinners and pies that come with a metal cooking dish that is discarded.

■ Don't buy aluminium foil for home packaging of foods. Let yourself run out; you will be able to get along without it. Use permanent, re-usable containers instead or wax paper.

■ Don't buy plastic or paper bags. You probably have a sufficient supply if you save the ones you get, without spending money for more.

■ Buy your ice cream in a cone instead of a discardable plastic dish.

See if you can re-use some of the containers you get

■ In Czechoslovakia and other East European countries, mustard, honey and other products come in glass containers made just like ordinary drinking glasses. Why don't we do this here? Try to think of uses for your glass jars. Start home brewing or pickling.

■ Soft plastic squeezy bottles from washing-up liquid can have various uses such as squirting your home-made cleaning fluids, watering home flowers or sprinkling dry clothes before ironing. You can think of more. Return them to the store you brought them from when you have no further uses for extra ones.

■ Try to buy in bulk, then you can transfer to the small more practical containers if necessary. Bulk containers are usually returnable or are more useful for paraffin or other materials.

■ Try making creative toys for children out of safe packaging, instead of buying expensive unimaginative ones.

■ Large tins or boxes can be decorated to make waste baskets for the degradable packaging you cannot find a use for.

Plastic packaging

Ten thousand tons of waste plastics are carelessly tossed away to litter streets and countryside. Unfortunately the properties which make them most useful for packaging, such as durability and unbreakability, also mean that they practically last forever when thrown away and continue as an unsightly mess and a hazard to rural animal life indefinitely.

The plastic manufacturers pretend to show great concern over these problems by giving money to Keep Britain Tidy groups, or by helping to produce technical solutions to the gases discharged from incinerators which burn plastic waste.

Most of these are minor publicity exercises which at best treat the effects rather than the causes, and which ignore the vast amounts spent on promoting the very attitudes which increase littering and waste. Meanwhile attempts to do research into light-degradable plastics, such as at Aston University in Birmingham, have to close down through lack of funds. Too little is known about bacterial decay to know why bacteria do not attack plastics. Three-layer plastic is perhaps a possibility. The outer two layers would be stable until the container is smashed; then chemicals contained in the inside layer could start breaking down the other two layers on exposure to the air.

The most promising approach, though, seems to be the degradability of substances already added to plastics. These substances are anti-oxidants which prevent the long chain plastic molecules from breaking down. If the anti-oxidant could be degradable then the plastic would also break down over time.

The development of a range of plastics with different degradable properties according to their use might need government subsidy or tax, due to the high development costs involved. However, if packaging increases to four times the present amount by 1980, as estimated, then degradable plastics will become an environmental and social necessity. Developing ways of recycling plastics would also provide part of the answer.

LITTER

Litter is a result of our slovenly throw-away attitude encouraged by 'disposable' goods. It is also an attitude that has to change. Don't litter. It's as simple as that. No one appreciates litter on the landscape. Keep Britain Tidy Group estimates that more than £20 million a year is spent on litter collection.

Show your respect for the land by making sure that you make no contribution to the litter that despoils it.

- Carry a litter bag in your car and use it.
- Make sure that rubbish cannot escape from your dustbin, even on a windy day.
- Never dump rubbish illegally; report any violations of dumping that you see.
- Be willing to pick up other people's litter. If you have the courage, retrieve litter and return it to the litterbug on the spot. You can ask him if he 'forgot' to pick it up himself.
- Participate in clean-up campaigns and help to organize them.

CHRISTMAS

One of the best single illustrations of the way we have lost our sense of proportion is our consumer behaviour at major religious festivals such as Christmas. It is at holiday times like these when we should reflect on our humble place in the universe, instead of turning them into orgies of waste and consumption.

The place is strewn with tinsel, paper, packaging and other junk, and the overloaded dustbins clog up the disposal system for weeks during the 'party' season.

Christmas should be a happy time but it can be even more fun without the unnecessary excess. Parents and children can work together for weeks making their own decorations. Many magazines give ideas for these, and for other home-made cards and presents too.

You can plant a live Christmas tree instead of buying a dead one. Each year millions of pine trees are cut down in which the yearly quest for the perfect Christmas tree usually produces a less-than-perfect specimen, chopped down several weeks earlier and ready to drop its needles and become a fire hazard.

The alternative is to buy a modest-sized pine which can be bought live and kept for several years in a tub of sufficient size. You should consult with a local nursery about the proper choice and care. Each year it can be brought indoors for a week or two during the Christmas season, and when it grows too large, it can be planted on one's own property or donated to the municipal parks department.

3. POPULATION AND FOOD CONSUMPTION

3 POPULATION AND FOOD CONSUMPTION

POPULATION AND THE QUALITY OF LIFE

A great debate has developed over the question of how much of the 'blame' for the deteriorating quality of our environment should be assigned to overpopulation, and how much to failures of our social systems and technology. On the one hand is the faction that tends to trace most of the problems to the simple fact that more and more people are putting demands on our planet's finite resources. On the other is the group which believes that most of our problems can be solved by technology and social engineering. They do not feel that we have reached the limits of our resources. They tend to ascribe our problems to weaknesses in our social, industrial, and governmental structures – all of which can be solved with some rearrangement of priorities.

The differences of these two points of view are important primarily because of the different sorts of solutions that their proponents propose. The weakness of both positions is that advocates of each tend to spend unfortunately large amounts of time and energy defending their point of view *against* the other – for example, birth control *versus* technical solutions.

Both views have important points to make which cannot be ignored, and it makes sense to adopt those strategies from both sides which point towards survival in a better world.

This does not, however, affect the fact that we will face very real problems of relating the number of people to the resources available. More people means more pollution – and less land, less resources, less space and less freedom for each new individual that comes along. We must realize that the Earth has its limits and budget accordingly. We can trade our resources or skills with someone else, we can find substitutes for many materials or we can develop processes and technologies which allow us to do more with what we have – but we cannot expand the basic capacity of the planet Earth.

Technology, even in the form of contraception for instance, provides some solutions to population limitation, but it is largely social, religious, and economic attitudes that have to change.

Overpopulation is normally thought of as someone else's problem, and developing countries are especially urged by the rich industrial nations to curb their population growth. The truth though, is that the average Briton has a far more significant impact on world resources than the average Indian for instance. Each Briton consumes in a lifetime about 15 times as much of the Earth's finite resources as the average Indian. And all our policies and attitudes at the moment are designed to *increase* the gap between the ever-expanding consumption rate of a minority – grouped in North America, Western Europe and Japan – and the undernourished majority living in the rest of world.

Britain's population is expected to increase to 66.5 million by the year AD 2000, or 19 per cent up on the present 56 million. In the next thirty years these extra people will need an increase of two 650-pupil schools per week. And they will need 30 new towns the size of Nottingham. Urban and industrial expansion is expected to cover an area equivalent to Cornwall and Devon combined.

Britain is already one of the most crowded countries in the world (600 persons per square mile compared with China's 200 per square mile and USA's 55 per square mile). Density is more than double the national average in South East and North West England and emigration is unlikely to provide any long term answers.

Population limitation will occur at some point. This is an ecological certainty, but the longer we delay voluntary limitation, the more likely severe restraints will be imposed by governments in a panic.

Unfortunately the stabilization of population may not be achieved by family planning alone. Family planning is more concerned with the spacing of children rather than the limiting of numbers that people want. Nor will a drastic reduction in unwanted children by widespread use of contraception achieve the goal. To persuade people not to have the children they want is going to be a much more difficult proposition and really requires greater social and economic incentive.

There have been numerous suggestions including tax benefits for the single, more work for married women, increased pensions for childless old people, and withdrawal of family allowances after two children – all designed to discourage future births while providing safeguards for the present children of the poorest families. Social incentive may also come from the fact that all of us pay for children through our taxes – those who willingly have smaller families or no children may not be willing to pay for others to have as many as they like. It has been calculated that up to the age of sixteen, each child of a father paying standard rate tax receives the following payments:

Payments and remissions (Maternity Grant, Family Allowances and Tax Allowances)	£1,043
Services given by the State such as maternity services, education and youth services	£1,502
Total	£2,545

This is only the bare minimum. Each extra year at school costs £300, and this rises to £1,100 for each year spent in higher education. It doesn't stop there of course, and various services are needed for the rest of your life. Each prevented birth would thus save £2,000 almost immediately in education, family allowances, and other costs. The cost to

the taxpayer of providing free advice and contraceptives
would be a very small proportion of this saving.

Stop at two

While society's goal is not to limit the number of children
per family to two, its interest clearly lies in controlling the rate
of the population growth so that the country can live within
the limits of its resources and the capabilities of its social
institutions – something which the United Kingdom now
fails to do. The family that willingly has a large number of
children is clearly placing a large burden on society – a
morally questionable act. Either others must forgo having
children or the collective load is increased. In this respect,
families that can 'afford' many children tend to be the worst
offenders; for their children, raised affluently, will consume
more and waste more than the average.

Proper safeguards, however, must be made for children
already born, especially those from poorer families. This is
largely a matter of the rearrangement of social and political
priorities in order to reduce overall consumption and re-
distribute national wealth more fairly.

There are a large number of contraceptive techniques.
They range from abstinence, the rhythm method, and coitus
interruptus – which depend on will power and are less than
sure – to the use of the condom, diaphragm, intra-uterine
device (IUD), spermicide foam or jelly, and the Pill.
Abortion is beginning to be recognized as an acceptable
method of terminating unwanted pregnancy when contraceptive methods have failed to prevent it. And sterilization – vasectomy for the male, or tubal ligation for the
female – is the method of choice for a growing number of
people after their family has reached its planned size.

The method of birth control that is used should be a personal decision made by husband and wife. It is also a medical matter, and a doctor should be consulted whenever a
medical method is used. In practice, Church and State also
impose conditions that restrict the freedom of the couple to

decide for themselves. But attitudes are rapidly changing. The Roman Catholic Church is no longer monolithic in its opposition to any form of birth control. Many individual Catholics consider the question to be a matter of personal conscience. And nowhere are conditions changing more rapidly than over the question of abortion. It is interesting to note that in Japan abortion is the socially acceptable method of controlling births and the IUD and Pill are socially unacceptable: whereas in this country, the situation is precisely the reverse. On a world scale, abortion is also by far the commonest form of contraception despite strong social disapproval by certain groups of people. It would not be good, however, to encourage the attitude that abortion is the best method since obviously the ideal is not to reach that stage in an unwanted pregnancy. The burden an abortion places on a woman is something that should not be considered lightly by anyone.

The reader wishing to have more information on any particular method of birth control is referred to any reputable manual on marriage and birth control. Your doctor is another source of information. In addition the Family Planning Association, women's groups, and student services can usually supply information that is relevant to your locality.

Adopt the rest

If you want to have more children, adopt them. There are thousands of children who need the love that you can give. Investigate and find out whether you qualify to adopt a child. In some cases single adults, as well as married couples, can qualify. Ask friends who have adopted children, investigate through your church or local social services. A booklet on adoption procedures is available from the Consumers' Association.

The Family Planning Act of 1967 which allows local health authorities to set up family planning services is not compulsory, so many local authorities have been very slow in setting them up, and those established are usually poorly publicized. Find out if there is a clinic in your area, if not ask why?

You can urge your MP to lift the veil of secrecy on the Government's activities and attitudes concerning population planning and ask him to support any forthcoming legislation or reforms.

The Conservation Society in their excellent booklet *Why Britain Needs a Population Policy* gives a list of population issues where Government action is required. It is quite a list and illustrates how far our Government has yet to go:

■ The Government should recognize that the size of the population is a proper Government concern and that present circumstances in Britain warrant Government action.

■ That Government should adopt a comprehensive population policy whose main aim should be to stabilize the size of the population. This aim could probably be achieved by measures which would not only be acceptable to, but positively welcomed by, the large majority of people.

■ The National Health Service should have overall responsibility for family planning.

■ There should be the widest possible dissemination of objective knowledge of effective methods of birth control and easy access to impartial professional advice.

■ The 1967 Family Planning Act should be made mandatory and activated in Scotland.

■ Family planning clinics should be set up in all maternity hospitals and the restrictions on the provision of contraceptive advice by hospitals removed.

■ All family doctors should be qualified to give contraceptive advice. Special courses should be arranged for doctors already practising who have not received training in contraception. In future all doctors who intend to enter general practice should receive such training as part of their postgraduate studies.

■ A domiciliary family planning service should be provided in all areas, or other suitable arrangements made, for mothers who might otherwise have difficulty in obtaining contraceptive advice.

▪ The Government should give financial support to the Brook Advisory Centres to enable them to expand their work for the unmarried.

▪ The distinction whereby contraceptive advice is available on medical grounds under the National Health Service but not on social grounds should be abolished, and contraceptive advice should be available free, the patient paying only the standard prescription charge.

▪ Family planning services should be widely publicized.

▪ All maternity hospitals should ensure that all women in their care are aware of the benefits of family planning.

▪ Health visitors should discuss with mothers of young children the benefits of family planning as a normal part of their work.

▪ The Government should take steps to ensure that the intention of the 1967 Abortion Act is not frustrated by lack of facilities or the unhelpful attitude of some doctors.

▪ Male sterilization (vasectomy) should be available on the National Health Service.

▪ All boys and girls should have an accurate knowledge of contraception by the time they leave school and be able to obtain professional advice on contraception.

▪ The Government should ensure that the public is aware that as the population grows Britain will progressively become a less pleasant country to live in and stress the social importance of family limitation.

▪ A Population Policy and Research Unit should be set up, directly responsible to the Prime Minister, to ensure that the Government and Parliament are kept fully informed about population trends and their implications.

POLLUTION AND HEALTH

The extent to which pollution affects our health is not fully understood, but it is clear that the effects are major.

Carcinogens (cancer-producing agents) contaminate our air and food, teratogenic pesticide residues deform foetuses, mutagens attack the genetic information we pass on to our children. Residues of chemicals that are used to protect our crops, additives that are used in our foods, and cosmetics we apply to our own bodies, all pose threats to health that are poorly researched and poorly understood.

Unfortunately there isn't much that we can do to protect ourselves against many types of pollution. In some cases the only thing we can do is run. And this is what a growing number of people, especially those with chest ailments, are advised by their doctors to do.

Although pollution *is* everywhere there are still some areas that are relatively clear of it. This will not continue to be the case, however, if everyone merely tries to flee from pollution. We must stop and fight. The pollution that you generate will harm someone else even if it doesn't harm you. Protect yourself from self-inflicted pollution.

■ Don't use pesticides. Home exposure is dangerous and unnecessary.

■ Don't use cosmetics or prepared foods excessively.

■ Don't smoke. (At least try cutting down.) Smoking attacks your own body and pollutes the air others must breathe.

■ Eat healthful foods and keep yourself in shape by exercise.

DEATH

One of the most ecological ways of recycling our bodies back to the earth is used by the Parsees in India. They place their dead on a tall tower, called a Tower of Silence, and the vultures come along and pick the bones dry. At the other extreme are the advanced embalming techniques and the monolithic monuments in the form of pyramids, created for the dead Kings and Queens of ancient Egypt. A modern version exists in America where the blood of the corpse is replaced by a chemical solution to preserve the semblance of life in an elaborate coffin. You can also pay to have your body deep-frozen until a way is found of reviving 'dead' tissues.

If we all used these methods to dispatch our dead there would soon be little space left for those who are alive. Cemeteries take up space which is especially valuable in some urban areas. Cremation is obviously less demanding on our resources, but cemeteries can be managed so that they can serve other needs such as recreation, peace and quiet or the encouragement of wildlife.

WHERE DOES THE MONEY GO?

Besides limiting the size of your family you can make a personal contribution by reducing your consumption. The sum of all your little actions will be significant and this book is intended to show what you can do.

First let's take a look at how our personal consumption is broken down.

Table 3. Consumers' expenditure 1969

	£ million
Household expenditure on food	5,977
Alcoholic drink	1,824
Tobacco	1,694
Housing	3,590
Fuel and light	1,421
Clothing	2,417
Durable goods	1,957
Other household goods	839
Books, newpapers and magazines	420
Chemists' goods	422
Miscellaneous recreational goods	637
Other miscellaneous goods	359
Running costs of motor vehicles	1,518
Travel	924
Communication services	284
Entertainment and recreational services	472
Domestic service	149
Catering (meals and accommodation)	1,477
Others	2,254
TOTAL	28,635

Source: *Annual Abstract of Statistics 1970. No. 107.* Central Statistical Office. HMSO.

This presents only a rough guide, but the magnitude of some items – cars, tobacco, alcohol, food, clothing, and housing – testify to the enormous market that exists for consumer goods. To a large extent though, responsibility for reducing environmental deterioration rests with the affluent, since they are by far the major consumers – and are often the managers and perpetuators of our system of over-consumption and waste.

FOOD

So many environmental issues come up when you shop for food that it is impossible to do justice to all of them in a few pages. Nevertheless, this section will attempt to cover most of the important issues in enough depth so that you can begin to devise a personal strategy for environmentally sounder living.

A large supermarket will probably stock a few thousand, *different* food items. In addition, there is usually a wide selection of paper products, laundry and cleaning aids, pest controls, and toiletry articles.

The market is a façade for the vast network of middle men who take the grain, fruit, vegetables, and meat from the farmer, the wood from the forester, and other raw materials from the primary producers, and process them into finished goods. If you are environmentally concerned, you care about what happens before the finished product reaches the market. It is the manufacturing and processing of many of the available goods which create environmental problems. Some products, especially some foods, are so adulterated by the time they reach the market that they actually constitute a hazard to health.

Most of the health hazards of foods, though, are beyond the scope of this book since additives, preservatives, and other chemicals do not originate from environmental sources but are added directly in the food-manufacturing process. (For information on these issues refer to *Brave New Victuals* by Elspeth Huxley.) It is largely the uninvited chemicals (by the manufacturers at least) that constitute an environmental hazard. These have probably entered the food through a biological food-chain system which concentrates the poisons in certain animals or plants, or have been deposited on food from the air.

Back on the farm

Farming is big business. Its raw materials are land, water, seed, animals, and fertilizers. Its job is to turn out food – as much as possible.

In fact in 1969 British farmland yielded 3,106,000 tons of wheat, 5,010,000 tons of barley, 893,000 tons of beef, 2,648,000,000 gallons of milk and 1,045,000,000 eggs (not counting those kept back for hatching). In 1946 the average yield of wheat was 19.1 cwt per acre: in 1969 it was 28·2 cwt. The barley yield rose from an average of 17·8 cwt per acre in 1946 to 27·4 cwt in 1969. All other produce has shown a similar increase. Modern agriculture has developed techniques including a large kit of chemical tools – fertilizers, defoliants, pesticides, and so on. Like any large industry, agriculture has also relied heavily on mechanization and on concentration of crops.

The result on the English landscape has been drastic. Especially noticeable are the large number of trees and hedges that have been uprooted at the rate of 5,000 miles a year to make larger fields, thus enabling larger machines to be used, sometimes three or four abreast.

Large areas of agricultural land are under intensive production of a single crop and every square yard of the field is ploughed. This has meant that chemical pesticides are needed to reduce loss of production and chemical fertilizers are needed to boost it.

Animal manure no longer returns to the soil to replenish the nutrients taken out by the harvest. It is cheaper to transport chemical fertilizer. The manure, therefore, ends up in the river, which it pollutes, and the fertilizer comes from a polluting factory or phosphate mine.

This continued intensification of crop production puts great pressures on the soil. The soil requires care and nourishment and its rate of recovery cannot be speeded up like tin cans on a conveyor belt. A recent Ministry of Agriculture report showed that the soil is at last breaking under the strain. In many parts of Britain it has been pushed to its limits and the structure is being destroyed by compaction, erosion and loss of organic content.

Intensification of crop production has other consequences too. Wind erosion has occurred where trees were removed. Hedges and ditches also affect drainage and water table levels and their removal increases evaporation from the soil.

Meanwhile the animals are confined in crowded, unhealthy feed lots. To prevent the outbreak of disease, their food is laced with antibiotics. This practice has the effect of contaminating the meat. It has another effect that is probably worse: the stomachs of cattle are breeding grounds for antibiotic-resistant strains of bacteria, some of which infect man. Thus, the routine use of antibiotics on animals is rendering these drugs ineffective in both animals and man.

In summary, the farmer, who should be a self-trained ecologist, has become instead an industrial manager who knows very little about the process he is managing. Thus the food industry may eventually lead to the destruction of the very basis of our long-term food supply – the soil.

Uninvited additives

These may more accurately be called contaminants. The most pressing problem is with the persistent pesticides, mainly DDT derivatives and other chlorinated hydrocarbons, such as aldrin and dieldrin. Because of their persistence and chemical properties, these chemicals tend to get more concentrated the higher up the food chain you go. The cow eats grass, she collects the DDT from the grass and concentrates it in her milk. Humans drink the milk and collect still-higher levels in their fat. Similar concentration takes place in fish and wildlife.

There is now a voluntary ban on the widespread use of these persistent insecticides, but the chemicals from previous use are still being concentrated in the food chains and are being drained from the soil into our seas and oceans.

Mercury is another pollutant that has been found at high levels in fish. Recently, large consignments of tuna fish were confiscated in the USA because of their high concentrations of mercurial compounds. The source of most mercury has been industrial waste, notably from paper and pulp production. The Baltic sea, which is lined with Scandinavian paper industries, contains high levels of mercury pollution in certain areas. Agriculture contributes a significant share of mercury to the environment as well. Seeds treated with mercurial fungicides have been known to reach man by way of game birds.

There is also concern over the amount of hormones and antibiotic residues that survive from intensive livestock rearing, to contaminate our supply of meat and milk.

Other unintentional additives can migrate into foods from their packaging, for instance plasticizers from plastics, fillers in paper and cardboard, and glue and adhesives. Like food additives, packaging is regulated, but safety is less than assured. Like the growth in additives, the growth in modern food packaging is moving us in directions that create more potential hazards, not less.

Shopping for a defensive diet

Overwhelmed by an immense array of environmental issues behind almost every item of food you buy, there are two attitudes you could take.

The first is a somewhat defensive one. The objective is to protect yourself and the environment around you from all of the hazards that man has created. The problem with this approach is that it is terribly easy to become overwhelmed.

The second approach is more optimistic. You place faith in the ability of your own body and in the capacity of the Earth's ecosystem to absorb the insults that are thrown at them. You seek to understand how these systems work and how man's technologies work; and you try to minimize the insults to the things you value to the greatest extent that you can. The problem with the second approach is that it is terribly easy to lose concern.

Rather than take one of the two extremes, as many people will do, you should try to combine concern for survival with a faith that your contribution can make a difference.

Some of the issues, such as packaging, have been dealt with in other chapters but here are a few directions on where to start.

Home preparation and preserving

This gives you greater control over the source of food and exactly what goes into it. Home gardening and home preserving are the best ways to assure that your food is free from pesticide residues and additives.

■ Make it a policy to buy fresh foods, especially during the summer when they are available. Simply avoid buying frozen and canned food if you possibly can. Any decent cookbook will tell you how to prepare fresh foods that will taste more appetizing and be more wholesome. In this way you can also cut down on your contribution to packaging waste. You can prevent the pollution that occurs during the mechanical processing and extended storage of commercial foods. If it is prepared in your own kitchen, you have control over the waste and can see to it that it gets put on your compost pile.

■ If you feel ambitious or even just a little adventurous, you should investigate home preserving. You should time your efforts to coincide with the harvest, when produce is plentiful and cheap. Then, with a stock of re-usable jars, lids, and a cooker, you can put by enough to supply you through a good part of the winter.

■ Gardens and stores are not the only places that you can find food. With a knowledge of plants, you can find a banquet of berries, greens, roots, and other natural foods in any unsprayed field or forest. It isn't wise to go foraging without some knowledge of plants, because there are poisonous plants mixed in with the edible ones. There are several good books which provide information and recipes on wild foods.

REDUCING FOOD COSTS

Ways of reducing your food costs will often reduce the environmental impact of food production.

It is commonly believed that you have to pay a lot more to eat wholesome natural foods. This is usually not the case. If you live in a city and your only source of organic food is a natural food store that must import all of its food, then that food will cost more. If you try to buy fresh strawberries during winter, they will, of course, be very expensive – if you can even find them. In season, however, most fresh produce is priced near or below the cost of processed equivalents. If you can deal directly with the grower, the costs are likely to be quite low, for there are no middle men and no promotional or packaging expenses to put up the cost.

Growing your own food or collecting it free in a field, at the seashore, or from a stream is least expensive. It has been suggested that an acre of suburban garden is much more productive than an equivalent area of farmland.

Another way to reduce the cost of your food is to eat only enough meat to get the protein you need and no more. It takes considerably more land and water to raise an animal than it does to grow an equivalent weight of vegetables. A mature steer eats 25 to 35 pounds of grass each day and defecates 6 to 25 pounds of manure for each pound of weight gain. In the future, as pressures on agricultural production continue to grow, meat will become progressively more expensive; and vegetable protein, supplemented as needed with the essential amino acids, will gradually displace meat protein. It is happening today – witness the ubiquitous soya-bean protein and hydrolysed vegetable protein on so many food labels.

Industrial food manufacturing often increases the cost of the end product against the cost of raw material many times. This is especially so of the many 'convenience foods' on the market. You may also lose out in taste, increased packaging and nutrition by putting convenience first. Be willing to put 'convenience' in its proper place.

ALTERNATIVES

There are lots of alternatives to commercially prepared, chemically laden foods. Here are some suggestions.

■ Instead of frozen or tinned fruit juices, have the real thing. Eat an orange or grapefruit for breakfast.

■ Instead of buying a fizzy drink, make your own lemon squash. Squeeze a lemon and add water and sugar to taste.

■ If it's a diet drink you crave, try the ultimate (no calories) – water on crushed ice.

If the situation with *intentional* additives is not good, the problem with *unintentional* additives is even worse. To protect yourself from pesticide residues in food, you can do the following:

■ Eat low on the food chain. This means a diet of vegetables and fruits primarily.

■ Wash all fruit and vegetables before you eat them. Some say that the skins of fruit such as apples should not be eaten to avoid sprays, but this skin is also where some of the vitamins are concentrated.

■ Be willing to accept fruit and produce that is less than perfect. A blemish is certainly preferable to a load of poison. Non-perfect produce may also be bought cheaper.

■ Grow your own food without pesticides, or buy from organic food stores.

■ If farmers in your area sow seed treated with mercurial fungicides, any wild game you shoot may not be safe to eat. Avoid eating it.

■ Don't eat fish that comes from inland waters unless you know the source to be unpolluted.

■ Reduce your consumption of the fat parts of meat, for

this is the place where the persistent hydrocarbon insecticides tend to be concentrated.

■ Of course, you should never use any pesticide around
food. Exposure to pesticides by this route can render in-
significant all other protective measures.

The pesticide residues that men and women carry in the
fat of their bodies is acquired by eating pesticide-laden
foods over a long period of time. In fact, since the residues
can cross the placental barrier, even newborn babies start
out with DDT in their bodies. You will not be able to
eliminate pesticides from your diet altogether because contamination is so widespread, but a low-pesticide diet will,
over the long run, lower the amounts of pesticide residues
your body has to carry.

Table 4. Estimated household food expenditure and consumption in Great Britain, September 1969–September 1970

Item	ounces per head per week
Liquid milk (pints)	4·70
Processed milk, and cream (pint equivalents)	0·43
Cheese	3·56
Butter	5·91
Margarine	2·87
Other fats	3·08
Eggs (number)	4·65
Carcase meat	15·88
Bacon and ham, uncooked	5·25
All other meat	18·28
Fish	5·38
Fresh fruit	23·00
Other fruit	7·20
Potatoes	50·97
Fresh green vegetables	12·94
Other vegetables	22·51
Bread	38·09
Flour	5·58

T–C

Table 4 contd.

	ounces per head per week
Cakes and biscuits	11·34
Other cereals	7·90
Sugar	16·82
Preserves	2·60
Tea	2·56
Other beverages	1·05

Source: Ministry of Agriculture, Fisheries and Food (National Food Survey).

4. START WITH WHERE YOU LIVE

4 START WHERE YOU LIVE

Concern for the environment starts with where you live. It is through the home and its immediate surroundings that you can have the most direct influence on your local environment.

LAND USE

The reasons for continually re-thinking our land use policies are compelling. Responding to the desires of millions of consumers, we have already carved up thousands of acres of land into housing estates set in a sea of asphalt and concrete. This 'suburbanization' has devoured prime agricultural lands and has threatened marshlands and estuarine areas that are vital for renewing the ecological cycles that support commercially important marine life. It has robbed urban dwellers of contact with natural open space, and has meant increased reliance on the private car for transportation.

Another development in the housing market has been a move towards multiple dwelling units in new housing construction. High-rise apartments can be built at lower per-unit costs and they permit centralization of facilities such as laundries and refuse disposal, and leave open space for public recreation and conservation uses. This is in *theory* anyway. They also cause social and psychological problems, and, in the case of Ronan Point, real physical danger. Too often the open space between the tower blocks is unimaginatively designed or filled with parking spaces. There must be a suitable compromise to achieve a more human scale of building with economic and aesthetic use of space.

If you decide that you are still in the market for a private home, then keep some of the following factors in mind:

■ Houses that are built on platforms carved out of hill-sides or in the flood-plains of rivers are more vulnerable to natural disaster.

■ Houses that are built in low areas, or near water, are more likely to have insect problems.

■ Houses in a sheltered valley of an urban area tend to get more pollution since the valley acts as a funnel and traps the polluted air.

■ In a basement or ground-floor flat near a main road, pollution may be ten times as much as in the rest of the town.

■ Houses downwind from a factory or industrial area sometimes suffer heavy pollution. In Britain the cleanest side of an industrial area is usually the western side, unless you live right next to the source.

■ Most prime agricultural lands and marshlands have a higher value to modern society as farms and as marshes than as housing estates, even if their real-estate pound evaluation is high. Suitable alternative locations for housing usually exist elsewhere, not so for the farms or marshes. Don't be a party to misuse of such land.

■ Open space in a congested area is valuable. If overall housing density must be increased, it should not be at the expense of necessary parks and open corridors. Again, to the extent that you can stay away from improperly located housing.

■ Many older buildings can be made much more valuable by a relatively small investment in renovations. It is wasteful of resources to destroy structurally sound housing unless there is a very good reason to do so. The Government has realized this since new house building has fallen behind demand. Local government grants are now available for home improvements and conversions.

■ Homes that have trees and grass surrounding them are likely to be cleaner, cooler and quieter.

■ Some builders take greater pains to protect the valuable qualities of a building site (e.g. trees, soil condition, proximity of neighbouring buildings, etc). Shop around before you select a builder – look at examples of work in progress as well as finished products.

These land-use problems are difficult, and there is not much that you as an individual buyer or seller can do to influence trends. Your investment in a home or your monthly rent represents one of the largest components of your budget. You probably feel less free to make a totally rational decision for this reason. You should, however, keep in mind the fact that the decision on where you live has a profound effect on how much money you will spend on other items, on what the environmental costs of the spending of that money might be, and on the quality of your life.

SECOND HOMES AND HOLIDAY COTTAGES

For a long time there has been a group of people, admittedly
a minority, who get a lot of pleasure out of camping and
'roughing it' in the wilder areas, away from people and civilization. On the basis of their conservation activities, the
recent environmental awakening has grown. What has
become clear is that the fight to save our countryside is also
a fight to protect civilization, for both are threatened by the
same problems.

As we have become more affluent, greater numbers of us
have sought to escape the deteriorating urban and suburban
environments to experience some of the joys of the natural
world. We travel long distances and flood the seashores and
beauty spots to more than capacity. The need for more such
recreational facilities is pressing because of the limited
carrying capacity that natural ecosystems have. Over-use
means the destruction of the beauties that first brought
people to the area.

While it is only the few who own country cottages or
caravans by the sea, the growth in such housing has been
great.

■ If you have a country cottage, why not share it with
people or let it be used by children who might not otherwise
get a holiday?

■ If you are thinking of buying one, why not share its cost
and use it with several families?

DESIGN OF THE HOME

It shouldn't come as a surprise to anyone with an awareness of ecology that the elements that go into a successful housing design are many, and that they all relate one to another. Thus, the site, choice of materials, and design are properly co-ordinated so that the final product is aesthetically pleasing, as well as economic to build and maintain. It takes talent and training to carry out housing design as it should be done. It is unfortunate that very little of the talent that is available has been used to design housing for the general public. Monotonous acres of uniform suburbs and monolithic towers of council housing in cities are testimony to our non-concern.

No one should embark on the project of building a house without careful thought and planning. If and when you undertake such a project, keep in mind some of the environmental factors that are discussed in this book.

Most of us, though, will never build a home of our own. Everyone, however, exerts control to some degree over his shelter and the way in which it relates to the broader community interest. We re-model, we plant, we dig, we landscape, we maintain or we don't maintain, we deal with pests, and we buy large numbers of products that have impact on the quality of the environment that we and others experience. What follows looks selectively at some of these consumer decisions.

What should your house be made of?

There are, of course, many alternatives in the material used for housing construction. Pre-stressed concrete, metals, cinderblocks, and bricks are the most common, but plastics are used more and more in building construction. In plumbing, floor covering, insulation, panelling, and other uses where permanence is a virtue, well-made plastics have a definite place. Especially interesting is the growing list of building materials that are made from industrial by-products that were formerly thrown away or incinerated. Here are some examples:

▪ Most of the large slabs of wallboard you see are made out of 'waste' wood blocks, wood-chips, and sawdust, usually stuck together with resin.

▪ Calcium sulphate from spent pickling liquor in the steel industry and from inorganic sludges in the pulp, paper, and fertilizer industries, can be made into gypsum wallboard – under the trade name of *Gyprock*.

▪ Fly-ash from power industry furnaces has found a market in pre-cast and structural concrete and building blocks, and as a filler in cement and bricks. The Central Electricity Generating Board can tell you about their Pulverized Fuel Ash (PFA). CEGB, Information Service, 15 Newgate Street, London, EC1.

The Building Centre, 26 Store Street, London, WC1, can provide information on a variety of building material made from industrial waste.

Your home represents a major investment. It makes sense, therefore, practically and ecologically to take good care of it. A well repaired house will extend the life of all the raw materials that have gone into building it.

Heating your home

Heating equipment uses a large proportion of the energy that flows into your home. Home owners face a wide range of heating conditions and an equally wide choice of equipment. Normally the choice is made wholly on the basis of costs. But what are some of the environmental factors?

Heating efficiency. The job of most heating systems is to convert the energy that is stored chemically in fuels into heat. Thus, when you compare electricity with gas, coal, and oil, the starting point is always the fuel and the end point is the heat in your home. Because the various fuels burn with different outputs of heat, normal practice is to start with BTU's (British thermal units – the amount of heat needed to raise the temperature of one pound of water one degree Fahrenheit) of fuel energy.

For example, electric heating involves converting the heat content of the fuel into electrical energy, transmitting this energy to your home by wires, and converting it back to heat in a furnace, or through one of many types of individually controlled electric heaters. The first step is usually done with an efficiency of only about 35 per cent, and sometimes a lot less. Transmission and distribution losses vary – in a fairly compact urban area they are about 7 per cent. Thus, though conversion of electric energy to heat in the home appliances may be 100 per cent efficient, the overall process is only about 30 per cent efficient, or less. The more efficient the conversion in the furnace, the less fuel energy reaches the atmosphere as waste heat and unburned fuel. Waste heat, though, is no problem. Oil and gas have a greater efficiency over electric heat which is offset to some extent by the distribution costs of the fuel.

Pollution and heating. All power pollutes. The open coal fire has obviously been the greatest cause of air pollution, covering buildings, streets, and washing in black soot. Since the Clean Air Act of 1956, this form of pollution has been considerably reduced, along with the sulphur dioxide gases that were also given off. There are still some areas, however, where the Clean Air Act is not enforced and coal is still used. If you are in one of these areas press your local council to take action – you can also get a grant to convert your heating equipment to other forms of fuel.

Electric heat is not clean if you take into account the greater thermal pollution, the lower efficiency and consequent greater use of fuel, the gases that are discharged into the atmosphere from the power-plant chimneys, and the radiation pollution from nuclear power. Fossil fuels, too, must be won from the ground and transported, and that means mines, slag heaps, wells, and oil spills.

Exactly how you balance these environmental costs in your choice of a home heating system, though, is a rather subjective matter. Which pollution is worse depends upon a variety of local conditions, but regardless of the way in which you heat your home, you can reduce the adverse impact of your heating system on environmental quality. At the same time, you will save on heating costs.

■ Keep your equipment in good operating condition. In this way you can improve efficiency and reduce unburned fuel to a minimum.

■ One of the best ways of reducing heating requirements is by properly insulating your home. The first consideration should be to insulate the walls and roof. Only then consider double glazing, since in an ordinary house windows account for only 10–20 per cent of heat loss. It is much cheaper and more effective to insulate walls anyway. This can easily be done with double-walls which are found in most houses built since 1930.

■ A well insulated home will also stay cooler in the summer.

THE LAND AROUND YOUR HOME

There are many ways you can improve the environment through your own garden. Most of these ways, such as encouraging wildlife, are dealt with in a later chapter as with the environmental damage caused by pesticides and weed-killers.

PLANT TREES

Why not plant trees? Everyone seems to be pulling them up these days. A tree makes a marvellous gift for a wedding anniversary or some similar occasion.

Trees and plants are also great moderators. They soak up sound, break up the wind, and create cool shade. In a real sense, they are a non-polluting alternative to acoustic tile and air conditioning. Their roots absorb and hold moisture, while their leaves give it off. Their branches provide a home for birds and their fruit and seeds provide food for wildlife. Trees and green plants also participate in the biochemical cycle in which carbon dioxide and sunlight combine to make carbohydrates and oxygen. This chemical reaction is central to the whole fabric of life on this planet, for it produces almost all of our available energy. There is a romantic notion that planting trees measurably increases the amount of oxygen we have to breathe, and that killing all green plants and the green algae and phytoplankton of the sea would bring about the suffocation of man, but this argument is not backed up by the facts. Plants consume the same amount of oxygen when they decay or are eaten, as they produce while growing. Furthermore, based on what we know of fossil fuel reserves and the stocks of hydrocarbons stored in living plants and animals, all of these could be burned without reducing the oxygen content of the atmosphere by one per cent. Oxygen comprises 20 per cent of the atmosphere.

A problem does exist, however, with carbon dioxide, which makes up less than one per cent of the atmosphere. There is great concern that increasing the concentration of carbon dioxide in the atmosphere can have considerable effects on the climate. The 'green-house effect' tends to increase the temperature here on earth by trapping solar radiation. CO_2 levels are up 15 per cent since 1890 and are expected to be 30 per cent higher than now by the year AD 2000. The reduction of the total amount of vegetation on the Earth does raise CO_2 levels; the burning of fossil fuels, however, is far more significant.

Growing anything, especially in the city and suburbs, requires at least a little forethought. If you are creating a landscaping scheme for your home, trees and shrubs should be selected with scale and proportion, and even pollution, in mind. They should be placed to create shade and to be shaded as needed. One should also keep soil conditions and, in urban and industrial areas, air pollution, in mind. To get complete, accurate information relevant to your situation, contact a local nursery, garden club, or landscape architect.

Keep both aesthetics and ecology in mind. Design diversity into your scheme, for diversity is what helps to stabilize natural systems. It is also important that the species you choose will be able to thrive, for healthy plants resist pests and weak ones attract them. You can plant to *attract* birds and squirrels *or* to keep them away, bearing in mind that birds help to control insects.

The *Architects' Journal* has produced a series of factual articles on landscaping around buildings, with lots of useful information on siting, planting, and maintenance of a variety of plants for particular purposes. These are to be produced in book form.

ENVIRONMENTAL HAZARDS IN THE HOME

Hazards have always been a part of man's world. It would be folly to believe that we will ever reach a time when this will not be the case. The heart of the situation is that as man gains knowledge of how the world works, he is driven by inborn curiosity to apply that knowledge in new ways. New applications breed new hazards, and the cycle is constantly renewed. At the same time, man's instinct for survival drives him to find ways to eliminate the hazards, or learn how to live with them.

We are still trying to learn how to live with our enormous supplies of power, our rapid transportation and communication, and the thousands of chemical tools that the technologists have placed in our hands. Thus environmental hazards are entering our lives at an incredible rate, but only a few of those that originate in the home can be dealt with here.

NOISE POLLUTION

Noise is pollution. It is an agent that decreases property values, creates physical damage, impairs hearing, impedes efficiency, and threatens the sanity of modern man.

Measuring noise

The unit of noise is the decibel (db). The threshold of hearing is at zero decibels. On the decibel scale a few levels are especially significant. Somewhere around 180 db is the lethal level. Rats exposed to 150 db first turn homosexual and cannibalistic and eventually are killed by heart failure. Short exposure to 150 db can permanently damage the human ear. The threshold of pain is around 120 db. Short exposure to between 100 and 125 db can cause temporary deafness and long-term exposure to anything over 80 db invites hearing loss.

Minimize noise at the source. Table 3 summarizes a variety of commonly experienced sounds – you meet some of them at work, in your home, out of doors, and when travelling. You have control over many of them, especially those in the home. Do what you can to stop this noise at the source. Just sit and listen to all the various sources sometime and see if you can trace them.

▪ The kitchen, living room, and play or work room are the noise centres of the home. Kitchen appliances, such as food mixers and dishwashers can raise the noise level to over 100 db. Noise is one more reason for minimizing your use of these machines.

▪ Noise-test any appliance before you buy it. Manu-

Table 5. Common Noise Levels

The threshold of hearing	0 db
The danger level	80 db
The threshold of pain	120 db
The lethal level	180 db
Jet aircraft at 200 feet	150 db
Pneumatic riveter, air raid siren	130 db
A 'hard-rock' band	115 db
Power mower, accelerating motorcycle	110 db
Food mixer (2 to 4 feet away)	100 db
Underground train	100 db
Heavy city traffic	90 db
Diesel trucks at 50 feet	68–99 db
Passenger cars at 50 feet	65–86 db
Loud shout at 1 foot	88 db
Normal conversation	60–70 db
Limit for phone conversation	60 db
Quiet street, average urban interior	50 db
Quiet room, residential area at night	40 db
Tick of watch at 2 feet	30 db
Whisper	20 db
Leaves rustling in the wind	10 db

Source: 'Noise Pollution, an Introduction to the Problem and an Outline for Future Legal Research,' James C. Hildebrand in *The Columbia Law Review*, Vol. 70, April 1970.

facturers have varying degrees of success in making their products quiet. In general, the more powerful the machine, the more noisy it is likely to be.

■ An appliance can be made less noisy by placing it on a sound-absorbent pad.

■ The television set introduces an enormous amount of noise into the home. Keep it under control. Watching the picture distracts most people from the sound volume even when they would soon notice a radio at the same volume.

■ Allegations have been made that consumers will not buy vacuum cleaners and other appliances that do not sound powerful. It is up to you to prove this is not so.

▪ There is a reasonable limit on power for music systems. The acoustic power output of a full orchestra seldom rises above 10 watts. Unless you aspire to follow Beethoven into deafness, there isn't much reason to equip your living room with hundreds of watts of audio power.

▪ If you want to take up an instrument, pick one that doesn't have a plug and an amplifier attached.

▪ Some heating systems are quieter than others. Water pipes can gurgle, steam pipes knock, and electric resistance heaters crackle.

▪ Plumbing can also be a source of noise and a means for transmitting it from flat to flat. Plastic plumbing has noise-insulating advantages.

▪ Noisy toilets can be fitted with a silencing tube which leads the water to the bottom of the tank instead of splashing at the top. The best device is the new Garston bell valve, developed by the Building Research Station.

▪ Dustbin noise can be bothersome, especially if the dustman comes early in the morning. Quiet rubber lids and plastic bins can be bought. Because of the problem of solid waste disposal, non-biodegradable plastic bags, though quiet, are less desirable and they cannot take hot ashes. Of course, reducing household waste will have the effect of reducing the number of bins you need to use.

▪ Buy a quiet lawn mower. Some power mowers have motors almost strong enough to drive a car. If your lawn is small enough, you should find a hand-propelled, reel mower entirely adequate and relatively quiet.

▪ Squeaky machinery can often be cured with a little bit of oil.

When defending your home against noise it makes sense to take steps to reduce the effect of unwanted noise as well as its sources.

▪ Inside the house, carpeting, acoustic ceiling tiles, and draperies all deaden noise. Acoustical ceilings can absorb between 55 per cent and 75 per cent of the sound energy striking their surfaces.

▪ You can add rolls of polystyrene sheeting to partition

walls. They go on just like wallpaper and can reduce damp
and conserve heat as well.

■ You can isolate noises by placing noisy appliances in
separate rooms.

■ The efforts you make to reduce heat loss from the home
may also help to reduce noise. Double glazing, to be effective
against noise, should be at least 7 inches apart, although 4
inches will reduce noise quite well if the wall between the
glass is covered with acoustic tiles.

■ Out of doors, trees serve the same sound-absorbing
function as drapes do indoors, while lawns are similar in
effect to carpets. Asphalt driveways and concrete patios, on
the other hand, cause noise to reverberate.

■ Noise falls off the further you are away from it (the
distance squared). Thus by doubling the distance between
yourself and the source, the noise diminishes by a factor of
four to six decibels.

Control your contribution to the general noise level:

■ Respect your neighbours by controlling the level of
noise that comes from your home.

■ Use your motor horn as sparingly as possible, and don't
slam car doors or rev-up engines unnecessarily.

■ Avoid taking aeroplane flights that are scheduled to take
off or land at night when they can disturb sleepers below.

Work to control public sources of noise

If the Concorde should ever become operational, boycott it.
Even if flights are restricted to 'non-populated' (by people)
areas, the sonic bang will be damaging and offensive. Wildlife and fish will still be adversely affected. Write to the
major airlines telling them of your intention to boycott the
Concorde giving your reasons. (You may be interested in
another Ballantine/Friends of the Earth publication, written by Richard Wiggs and titled *Concorde: The Case
Against Supersonic Transport*.)

Unfortunately, regulation of public noise is still in its in-
fancy. Support noise ordinances and report violators. Much
noise is avoidable.

CHEMICALS IN THE HOME

Hazardous chemicals are used in almost every household. Some of these chemical 'helpers' are immediately injurious or toxic, while many others have effects that are expressed more subtly. Cleaning products, polishes and waxes, wax removers, oven cleaners, disinfectants, room fresheners, cosmetics, insecticides, and other pesticides, and food additives all expose us to chemicals that can have detrimental effects on us if we do not take the appropriate precautions – and often even if we do.

Other chapters discuss some of the environmental problems associated with pesticides and food additives. The story with respect to the other products mentioned above is very similar. Regulation by government departments is poor, labelling information is frequently inadequate, and manufacturers show the same callous disregard for the safety of users of their products.

A large part of the reason that there are so many accidental poisonings and injuries is that many people never read the labels, or if they do, quickly forget or dismiss the warnings. This, in turn, is a result of the attitudes that advertising has engendered. Convenience, effectiveness, ease of use, pleasant odours, and cleaning power or killing power (for bugs), are emphasized with no mention of health risks at all.

What should you do?

Rather than dwelling on the hazards of each of the different chemicals, the following are some ideas of how to reduce the hazards and their adverse impact on the environment whilst still obtaining, through simpler alternatives, what these chemical wonders are supposed to accomplish.

Handle chemical products with care. The first rule is to handle chemical products with the care they deserve. Strong alkalies, such as potassium and sodium hydroxides and trisodium phosphate, and less-strong alkalies, such as washing soda, ammonia and borates, are commonly used in grease oven cleaners. Strong acids, such as hydrochloric and sulphuric acids, and the weaker acids in vinegar and lemon juice are used to remove hard-water deposits and metal stains. Bleaches are added to household cleaners to oxidize stains away. *It is most unwise to mix such cleaners.* The resulting cocktail may produce a substance that could seriously injure you.

▪ Anything with a 'keep out of reach of children' warning really should be kept out of the reach of children. It is wise to *lock up* hazardous chemicals.

▪ The products should be kept in their original containers so that the label can be re-read before each use. Ideally, such products should not be stored for a very long time.

▪ When scrubbing floors, walls, or windows with ammonia, or when spraying a room, windows should be kept *open* to provide good ventilation in the room.

▪ Strong alkalies and acids should not be used without wearing protective gloves.

Minimize use of harmful products. The best thing to do, however, is to try to reduce your use of the harmful products. For many of them there are perfectly acceptable alternatives which cost much less and which place much smaller demands on the environment.

▪ Window cleaners are an example. A solution of one tablespoon of household ammonia in a quart of water does as good a job as those that cost 15p or more. Furthermore, the water and ammonia mixture can be used in a refillable squeezy bottle from washing-up liquids.

▪ Similarly, a damp cloth is adequate for most dusting jobs. The shiny surface that is considered fashionable now has not always been so. Cleanliness should be the object, not gloss. The cycle of waxing, de-waxing, and re-waxing is so unnecessary.

■ Soap and water are sufficient for many of the jobs for which strong disinfectants are now used.

■ Baking soda and washing soda are environmentally preferable to many all-purpose cleaners, and do the job just as well in most cases.

■ Clean out the coffee-pot or percolator by brewing a couple of cups of baking soda solution in it.

■ Room fresheners cannot take out stale odours – they only cover them up. Instead of spraying more junk into the air, freshen the room by ventilating it. Open the windows, get rid of any sources of undesirable odours, and bring in a bouquet of flowers.

5. LIQUID ASSETS

5 LIQUID ASSETS

It may seem strange that while water is one of the most abundant compounds on Earth, its availability and supply is a headache for every industrial country in the world.

Obviously most of the world's water lies in the oceans and seas, and only that which falls as rain is suitable for human use. Rainfall is unreliable in many parts of the world and its seasonal characteristics mean that complicated systems have to be devised to store it for use when supply is scarce.

In industrial countries like Britain we also demand a high degree of purity in our daily supplies. It is expensive to make the water pure enough for us to drink, yet we use it mostly for purposes which do not require high standards – such as washing clothes and transport of sewage. At the same time we pour vast quantities of poisonous wastes into our rivers and ground-water systems making them unsuitable for water abstraction.

BRITAIN'S WATER SUPPLY

The most important supply for our use in Britain is obviously the 16,000 million gallons (mgd) which fall daily as rain on the land and either enter the ground-water system, or are returned to the atmosphere through plants and evaporation, and to the sea via rivers, so completing the natural global water cycle.

We do not have a very high rainfall in Britain and the problem is complicated by the fact that most rain falls where fewest people live. You can see from any rainfall map that it ranges from 80–200 inches per year in upland Wales and Scotland to about 20 inches per year in South-East England.

This uneven distribution of water is the major factor in all water policies for Britain. The drier summer months and uneven distribution both mean that water storage is essential, and pipes, canals, and river systems must be used to deliver the water to where it is most needed. Everyday, 600,000 million gallons are piped directly into our homes. It is obvious that you use this water as you flush the toilet, wash your clothes or have a cup of tea, but it is less obvious that you also consume water when you buy a newspaper, switch on the light or eat fish and chips.

The food you eat costs water. Plants take in water through their roots and release it into the atmosphere by transpiration. The water cost for a day's supply of vegetables and bread is around 200 gallons. Most industries, but especially the paper, food production, iron and steel, and chemical industries also use vast quantities of water. Although some of it becomes part of the product, most of the 300,000 million gallons per year used by industry goes out of the factory as waste water carrying a load of pollutants before it reaches a river or sewage system. In addition to the volume of industrial waste, industry throws into the water system poisonous chemical pollutants, such as mercury and other substances, that are non-biodegradable.

A complicating factor is the growing use of water for cooling purposes. Nuclear power plants use vast quantities to cool the steam used to drive the turbines. Although this does not add pollutants, heating the water removes oxygen thereby reducing the capacity of the water to degrade wastes. The heated water may also change the ecology of the rivers or estuaries into which it goes.

Additional contamination comes from pesticides residues, oil spillage, and agricultural fertilizer run-off. These all add to the burden that our freshwater system has to bear, not forgetting the other creatures that have to use the same water. Fish, waterfowl and shellfish that inhabit the inland rivers, lakes, and estuary areas also have a claim on clean water, too, as do the land animals that drink it.

We extract our present supplies from underground

sources, upland reservoirs, and from rivers, in roughly equal proportions. The total amount of fresh water practically available for use is about 10,000 mgd but at the present rate of increase demand will overtake the supply by AD 2000.

Large scale freshwater production from the sea is impracticable for the near future. And, given the controversy over nearly every upland reservoir, trying to double the supply from that source will become increasingly unacceptable. Barrage schemes for Morecambe Bay and The Wash have been proposed, and there are various other schemes for artificially replenishing underground sources, such as the aquifer under London. But there is no escape from the conclusion that it is the volume used, and the rate it is polluted, that must be reduced.

More and more of the waste water going into sewers must be purified at sewage works before it is dumped in our rivers. This is how London has to treat its waste water, since most of its water supply is extracted from the River Thames and its tributaries. Other cities such as Birmingham worry far less about where their sewage goes since fresh water supplies are piped from Wales. If the River Trent were not so dirty it could be used to supply sufficient water to make a major barrage schemes such the Wash unnecessary.

Although it sounds a fine idea to increase our water supply by cleaning up the rivers, the real snag is the indifference and ignorance of the general public. There really are no 'votes' in sewage treatment, and local authorities who are responsible for it give higher priority to new houses and industry which in turn place a greater burden on the sewage system.

Since our sources of water are limited and they are more scarce in the areas of greatest population, the only prospect is to conserve water supplies, increase re-use and recycling of water, and drastically reduce pollution. It is almost like having one pond to swim in, drink from, and throw all our waste into – pretty soon it will be of no use to anyone.

WATER CONSERVATION IN THE HOME

Today the average Briton uses about 45 gallons daily in the home. If you include the amount used indirectly by the consumption of industrial products it increases to something like 95 gallons per day. Not all of this is necessary as you would soon find out if it had to be pumped out by hand and carried back to the house as we used to do.

With limits on the amount of pure, drinkable water that can be made available it is about time we gave a little thought to ways of reducing the amount we use.

■ Repair all leaky taps and pipes. The steady flow wastes a considerable amount.

■ Don't run water unnecessarily. For example, don't keep the water running the whole time you are brushing your teeth. Don't leave hoses or garden sprinklers on unnecessarily.

■ Try the 'shower versus the bath' test. Take a shower and see how high the water level comes with the plug in the drain. If you use less water taking a bath, then take baths. If you can't stand the thought of losing your shower then reduce the amount of water used while showering by adjusting the nozzle to a finer spray or by replacing the shower head. You don't need the shower on the whole time either: try first wetting yourself, turn off the water, lather all over then turn on and rinse the soap off – it works just as well.

■ Like electric power, water use has periods of peak demands. Municipal water systems usually provide for at least double the average demand for maximum daily loads, and five times the average for hourly peaks. In residential areas where lawn watering is common in summer even these limits are sometimes exceeded. Water your lawn and confine other large quantity uses to non-peak periods.

■ Use all washing machines at full capacity. A dishwasher uses about 14 gallons, so don't turn it on every time you have three dirty plates. Scrape the plates and stack them in the washer until you have a full load. If you have no washer, leave single plates to soak until you have more – it will need less detergent and only additional hot water.

You do not really need a hose to wash the car. Use a bucket and sponge.

■ If you run the water while washing your hands you may use 2·2 gallons. Test yourself and get a bowl, or use taps which mix the hot and cold water.

CONSERVING MUNICIPAL WATER

The quality and efficiency of waste water systems must be expanded. Sewage treatment systems are vital – encourage your local authorities who are responsible for them. Write to them for further ideas on how to reduce water consumption and pollution. Show them you are really concerned and assure them that you would 'vote' for sewage treatment.

Encourage your municipality to employ tertiary treatment of its sewage. Primary treatment only settles out the solids. Secondary treatment gives the bacteria a chance to remove some of the oxygen demand but leaves the water nutrient-rich. Tertiary treatment removes these nutrients which should never have to be dumped into the water supply in the first place.

One of the best methods of waste water treatment is through land disposal, either by sprinkling or by irrigation. The wastes are broken down in the soil, where they act as a fertilizer, and the water soaks in to recharge the groundwater supply. Waste sewage water can be considered as misplaced fertilizer.

Protect groundwater

The protection of groundwater from pollution has many aspects.

■ Don't fill marshes and don't build on floodplains.

■ Avoid paving over areas as this increases the amount of water that runs off into the sewers and not into the ground. Forests act as reservoirs for water, releasing it slowly into streams and into the ground, so protect all forest areas if you can.

■ Never use pesticides in such a way that they could contaminate groundwater.

■ If you live in a suburb and have enough land and proper soil conditions, you should be able to use a septic tank. The septic tank consists of an underground basin where the sewage from your home is collected. There it is decomposed by bacteria. It also has a percolation system that returns the water to the groundwater system. Impurities are filtered out by the soil immediately around the tank. (Nevertheless, it is wise to locate the septic tank away from any wells.)

REDUCE YOUR SHARE OF INDUSTRY'S WATER USE

We have already indicated that the biggest polluters are food-processing, paper, chemical, and metal industries. Reducing unnecessary consumption in these areas will thus reduce your use of water.

■ Don't use coloured disposable paper products, especially toilet paper. The dyes pollute but the paper breaks down.

■ Reduce your consumption of electricity. In this way you can help lessen the thermal pollution load on waters.

■ Industry can drastically reduce the pollution burden it puts on surface waters. Industrial recycling of water and waste treatment will come if you apply pressure through government, and by publicizing the worst offenders.

To summarize, reduce your use of water and don't pollute. With proper management, there should be enough water to meet all of our needs – swimming, boating, and fishing included.

WATER FOR RECREATION

Freshwater lakes, reservoirs and canals provide opportunities for a variety of recreation activities, including boating, swimming, fishing, or just gazing.

Unfortunately the variety of possibilities can lead to conflict where incompatible activities are concerned. Swimming and boating often interfere with fishing, and noisy boats disturb the tranquillity of those interested in watching wildlife. Apart from this natural conflict some water sports create positive dangers, not just inconvenience. If you use water areas for recreation a Water Sports Code which gives guidance for proper conduct and safety, is available from the Central Council of Physical Recreation, 26 Park Crescent, London, W1.

Here are some ideas on promoting a better environment for those using water areas.

◼ Try non-powered forms of boating. Learn to punt or row instead. There should be certain areas that remain free from motorized living. Respect them.

◼ Don't throw litter overboard even if you are out at sea. Bring it back to land and dispose of it in the proper place. You can always tell a popular sailing or boating area by the amount of floating rubbish along the shore. For sewage, holding tanks are preferable to units that 'treat' the sewage on board then dump it overboard.

◼ Fuel spills are another hazard that boat owners should watch for.

Sea pollution

Tar on your sandwiches may be a familiar experience these days, but if you go down to some seaside places you may be in for a further surprise. The Belgian Consumers' Union has found that holidaymakers, swimming off the Belgian coast (English Channel) have a 12 per cent chance of contracting any of nine diseases known to be caused by sewage pollution. These include, conjunctivitis, ear infections, sinusitis, vaginitis, skin infection, enteritis, typhoid, para-typhoid and infectious hepatitis. In some places the rate of infection was as high as 23 per cent. The same study was undertaken on French, Spanish, and Italian coasts. In many coastal towns of Britain, sewage is pumped directly to the sea, yet no equivalent survey has been done here. Find out if the seaside town of your choice dumps untreated waste from its sewers into the sea.

REDUCING POLLUTION

Although the way we waste our water is important, it doesn't cause half as much trouble as what we put into it. Reduction of water pollution is a significant factor in ensuring a supply of sufficient pure fresh water for future demand. There are a few things you should remember.

■ Much of our sewage system is inadequate to deal with the wastes it is supposed to handle – so don't add any more burdens. Don't empty household or garden poisons, fertilizers or old medicines into the system. Waste oil, animal fat, and tips of filter cigarettes don't do it much good either.

■ There are safer and better ways to get rid of many of the things we carelessly flush down the loo.

DEAD LAKES AND OTHER WASHDAY MIRACLES

Synthetic detergents have been recognized as a cause of environmental pollution problems ever since their foam began turning up in our rivers in the early Sixties. More recently attention has been focused on the role of phosphates in detergents, causing increased algal growth in lakes and rivers.

The ever-changing chemical composition of detergents requires constant vigilance, but it is not just the chemicals themselves; it is the vast quantities that are used – some 550 thousand tons in 1970 – that is really causing the damage.

Our Ministry of the Environment watchdog, the Standing Technical Committee on Synthetic Detergents, has cautiously spelt out the gloomy prospects.

Last year [1969] we reported that the standard of river water quality, in relation to the concentration of detergents residues, had been maintained although we had been unable to make a reliable assessment of the extent of any permanent improvement. We now consider that there has been no further improvement and that in some respects there may have been some evidence of slight deterioration. The increased consumption of anionic and non-ionic surface active materials, if not matched by an increase in their biodegradability and the diluting effect of increased water consumption, could lead to a deterioration in the condition of our rivers. We are conscious that there has not been a 'dry' period of twelve months since the change-over to softer detergents for domestic use and we cannot rule out the possibility that the situation could become critical again and call for a reappraisal of our present attitudes to the detergent problem.

How detergents pollute

There are basically two types of detergents: soapy and soapless. The action of soapless or synthetic detergents is mainly what we are concerned with in this section.

The two principal ingredients of synthetic detergents are surface active agents (surfactants) and phosphates.

Surfactants. The surfactants are really what 'cleans' the clothing; they act by reducing the surface tension of water so that the dirt is loosened from the fibre. The surfactant molecule has two ends: the ionic end which attracts water and the non-ionic end which is attracted to oils and grease ('dirt'). These molecules surround the dirt particles forming what is called a micelle, thus making the dirt soluble in water. The surfactants used are usually sulphonated sodium compounds such as sodium alkyl benzene sulphonate. The presence of these chemicals in as little as 3 parts per million (ppm) makes life pretty miserable for fish – in fact so miserable for the more sensitive fish such as Trout that they die through the destruction of the membranes in their gills.

Most people have noticed detergent pollution, though – in the form of rafts of foam drifting down the local stream or river. Foam problems arose because the fatty end of the surfactant molecule was complex and branched. These 'hard' surfactants could not be broken down easily by the bacteria normally present in waste water and were thus non-biodegradable. They continued into the sewers and rivers building up occasionally into great walls of foam.

Since 1965 this problem has been reduced considerably by the development and use of simpler surfactants with un-branched molecules. In domestic detergents all but a very small proportion of surfactants are now biodegradable. It's a different story though with industrial detergents. About half of the industrial detergents are non-biodegradable and these are still a major problem for rivers located in concentrated industrial areas. We are still left with the horror of about 70 thousand tons of surfactants poured down the drain every year and this load on our water resources and sewage plants has increased sharply in recent years.

Although there has been a major change to more bio-degradable surface-active detergent ingredients there is little evidence that the total situation is getting any better and there is certainly no cause for complacency. The only answer seems to be to reduce our consumption, and this is where household use is important.

Phosphates. The phosphate component (usually in the form of sodium tripolyphosphate) makes up 25–50 per cent of the domestic powder detergents. These phosphates act as 'builders', increasing the performance of the surfactants. They also soften the water, and by increasing alkalinity break down oily and greasy soils, into minute droplets. They also prevent re-deposition of suspended dirt and reduce the number of germs in clothes.

The element phosphorus occurs naturally and is an essential nutrient for all living organisms. The recent tremendous increase in phosphates, from domestic detergents as well as chemical fertilizers and other sources, has had a marked effect on freshwater ecosystems especially in countries such as USA, Canada, Sweden, and Switzerland which have large bodies of standing water. Lake Erie, between the USA, and Canada, is by now a well known example of what can occur when increase in phosphates accelerates a process known as eutrophication. Almost all aquatic life has disappeared from Lake Erie and vast amounts of stinking algae get washed up on its shores.

Eutrophication is a natural process of the enrichment of lakes and ponds, and usually occurs over thousands of years, depending on the size of the lake. First the waters are oligotrophic (poor in nutrients and unable to support much aquatic life), then they are mesotrophic (with balanced plant and animal life), and finally they are eutrophic, where an over-abundance of nutrients causes rapid plant growth. The plants then die, and decayed plant material builds up at the bottom until the lake eventually becomes a marsh.

The primary effect of a rapid increase in organic waste when a water system is in the oligo- or mesotrophic stages is an increase in the amount of plant growth, especially algae, which were previously limited by the low phosphorus supply. These plants die off and the bacteria which normally break down organic waste in the water increase in population too. These bacteria require free oxygen as they reduce the dead plant material, and, with excessive food supplies, the oxygen which is vital for other aquatic life is used up. At this point another type of bacteria, anaerobic bacteria, which do not require oxygen, take over. Some of these anaerobes are sulphur bacteria which produce foul-smelling compounds such as amines and hydrogen sulphide, which has a smell like rotten eggs. Meanwhile sewage fungus grows at a rapid rate, reducing the light and air entering the water and causing plankton, fish, and other water creatures to die off.

The amount of phosphate needed in a detergent varies with the hardness of the water. A few products are formulated differently for different water conditions. Persil is one of these but all products should be. Areas with softer water require far less phosphate than those with hard water. Most manufacturers ignore this fact, instead adding enough softener to meet the needs of a broad market. Thus, your product may contain much more phosphate than you need.

There is some dispute, however, as to how severe increased eutrophication is in Britain and whether detergents are the main source of phosphate pollution. We have quite a few canals, ponds, and sluggish streams, and the rapid growth in detergent and fertilizer use doesn't give much cause for complacency. Every disturbance to water systems and every new chemical that gets dumped in the water, reduces its capacity to recover, and its usefulness for other purposes.

MORE WASHDAY WONDERS

Phosphate and surfactants are not the only contribution
synthetic detergents make to our battered water supplies.
Each detergent also has its fair share of bleaches, whiteners,
dyes, perfumes and other 'builders', as the manufacturers
euphemistically call them.

The bleaching action of detergents is done by chemicals
which oxidize stains such as tea. An increasing proportion
of the bleaching chemicals in packaged detergents are per-
borates – especially sodium perborate (about 15 per cent in
most packets – sometimes higher). At the moment, treatment of these chemicals in the sewage plants seems to be
ineffective and the boron element passes through into the
rivers where it could contaminate water re-used for drinking
purposes. Although boron in minute traces is an essential
element for plant growth, even in relatively low concentrations it becomes toxic. Boron may also become
concentrated in food crops, especially those which are
spray-irrigated with water supplies from contaminated
rivers.

Boron from detergents may not be a health hazard at present but the effects of increased proportions of sodium perborate in the powder, and increased use, could have long-
term consequences. Although boric acid is used as a food
additive it is now known that boron taken in large quantities
affects the central nervous system. Its effect on aquatic life,
by itself or combined with the considerable variety of other
new chemicals, can only be imagined at present.

AND FOR MY NEXT TRICK – ENZYME DETERGENTS

In the last few years a new detergent formula which includes an enzyme preparation has rapidly taken an important share of the household detergent market. Its higher price was supposed to be offset by certain advantages it had over conventional powders. These 'advantages' were skilfully played-up by claims of 'biological miracle' ingredients that 'digest' even the most persistent dirt and stains. Here at last was a genuine gimmick surpassing all the tired old adverts for the housewife who couldn't tell white from whiter than white.

Recently these products, dominated by Procter and Gamble's Ariel and Lever Brothers' Radiant, have come under suspicion for their ineffectiveness, their hazards to health, and their largely unknown effects on water systems and sewage treatment based on the 'biological' power of the enzymes.

Enzymes themselves are nothing new, nor are they little bugs that gobble up dirt and stains. They are chemical substances essential to every living organism and act to speed-up or catalyze most biochemical reactions. The enzyme used in detergents is one which is able to speed up the breakdown of complex protein molecules, which occur in substances such as blood, egg, gravy, etc, into simpler more soluble products. These proteolytic enzymes, as they are called, have been known for years and were first developed for cleaning purposes around 1913. Their recent use in detergents has been made possible by the development of mass-production techniques extracting the enzymes from a special type of bacteria called *Bacillus subtilis*.

The continuing activity of the enzymes is dependent on the conditions under which it is used – in this case on the temperature of the water and the other chemicals in the detergent. Most enzymes are unlikely to be very active above 65°C and this makes them rather ineffective in a hot cotton wash for instance. This is why the cooler pre-soaking is emphasized. On the other hand, common detergent ingredients such as sodium perborate bleach, work best at temperatures *above* 60°C besides inhibiting the enzyme action chemically.

The amount of these enzymes entering the environment has increased drastically with the introduction of new detergent brands, but the amount going into the water system is very difficult to estimate and may range from approximately 500 tons to well over 1,000 tons. The case against them as pollutants, though, is not great. In fact they are able to do the same job of breaking down organic waste that the sewage treatment plants are built to do.

Even though there may be no cause for concern as to their effect on the water and waste disposal systems, the health hazards are measurable. Several complaints of severe skin disorders have been traced to enzyme detergents by Hallenshire Hospital in Sheffield, and in the USA special precautions had to be taken for dust control and ventilation after workers in enzyme detergent factories suffered from dermatitis and flu-like symptoms. Besides the possible environmental hazards there is considerable doubt as to their real effectiveness compared with non-enzyme detergents. According to WHICH?, the magazine of the Consumers' Association, the performance of the enzyme detergents is not much different from the non-enzyme detergents tested, which were Omo and Persil, provided the clothes were given the same treatment with both types of powders including an overnight soaking to loosen dirt and stains. It was the overnight soaking which made the difference, and this was more likely to be done with enzyme detergents since it was recommended on the packet. This also meant an increase in the use of powder since more detergent was needed to finish the job off after the overnight soak. The only real advantage for enzyme detergents found by the WHICH? tests was improved washing results for women's pants.

We are here mainly concerned with the environmental problems arising from products, but as is always the case with detergents, the high promotional costs, the confusion of changing prices, different sizes, and brand names, make it almost impossible for the housewife to get value for her money. In addition, with enzyme detergents we have to suffer hysterical promotion, higher prices, and increased and largely unknown environmental costs to our rivers – all for inflated profits and a cleaner pair of knickers.

HOW TO REDUCE YOUR CONTRIBUTION
TO THE DETERGENT PROBLEM

The major source of detergent pollution is pretty obvious –
it's you, and everyone else who washes clothes, scrubs floors
or cleans dishes.

There are two ways to tackle the issue – firstly find ways
of reducing the amounts you use, and secondly find the less
polluting alternatives among the products available.

■ The first thing you should do is make up your own
mind how clean is clean, and whether whiteness is really
what you need. The 'optical brighteners' added to detergents
merely absorb ultra-violet light and radiate it as visible white
light. It's more a matter of aesthetics than actual cleanliness.
In fact different cultures have different ideas of what is clean
white. In South America the detergent clean white is slightly
reddish, while ours has a bluish tint. Clearly the 'whiteness'
has nothing to do with cleanliness or sanitation – it's just a
gimmick that has been carried too far.

■ Don't buy enzyme detergents: if they disappeared
tomorrow it would make no real difference. The greater
amounts of detergent used per wash, as well as their com-
parative ineffectiveness amounts to some considerable con
as well as an added burden to the rivers. In the USA, Procter & Gamble and Lever Brothers have now stopped
adding enzymes to all their detergent brands since sales have
fallen off as American consumers have become worried
about the harmful effects on health and the environment.
Yet they will continue to be sold in British stores while consumers are prepared to buy them.

■ Pre-soaking with almost anything including plain water

will improve washing performance but the use of high-phosphate enzyme detergents will make only a trivial contribution to greater cleanliness. Most ordinary detergents recommend a pre-soak anyway but only for really difficult stains.

■ If most people stuck to the recommended quantities in the first place detergent pollution could be drastically reduced. Try transferring your detergent to a coffee tin and drop in a little measuring spoon.

Soap and soda

Soap still maintains a major share of the detergent market but it is losing ground to synthetic alternatives all the time. It began to be replaced in the early 1940s by a functionally similar surfactant, the action of which has already been described.

Soap was first used by the early Romans who discovered that the mixture of fat and ashes from animal sacrifices, mixed with a special kind of clay, got the dirt out of clothing. For centuries soap was made in the same way, by boiling lye and grease together to obtain the salts of natural long-chain fatty acids. It is now made principally by heating animal fats, including beef and mutton tallow, or vegetable oils such as palm kernels, coconuts, or soya-bean, with caustic soda.

Various brands of soap flakes have been on the market for some time. These include Lux which is almost pure soap, Persil and Rinso with about 50 per cent soap, Oxydol 45 per cent soap, and Fairy Snow which has 60 per cent soap.

Soaps are made from renewable resources such as vegetable oils, while synthetic detergents come basically from non-renewable crude petroleum, the limited supplies of which are already being consumed at a horrifying rate.

By switching back to soaps you will be reducing environmental problems in several ways:
1. You will tend to use less total quantity of washing

powder and less of the more damaging ingredients such as phosphates and 'hard' surfactants.

2. You will reduce the wasted effort and resources spent in the promotion of new synthetic detergent brands.

3. You will also be reducing the need for sewage treatment and water purification, the cost of which ultimately comes from your pocket anyway. In the USA a government committee recommended a tax on detergents so as to transfer the cost of water treatment from the community to the consumer of the product.

4. Besides all this you will be saving money.

If you live in a soft water area you can switch directly to laundry soaps. If your water is hard and you are having a problem with soap scum add a few tablespoons of washing soda. Experiment and use as little as possible of both soap and softener.

If you have been washing with detergents your clothes may be coated with detergent residues that will turn yellow when you first use soap and soda. To avoid this wash once with hot water and soda (4 tablespoons) to strip off the residue.

Soap used in the washing machine

There is no reason why soaps cannot be used efficiently in automatic washing machines. The following tips will be useful when changing over:

One problem that inexperienced soap users can encounter is caused by soap reacting with minerals in hard water, forming a 'bath-tub ring' – an insoluble 'curd' which sticks to fabrics. This is difficult to rinse, and if left on fabrics will eventually give a grey appearance to the clothes. Such a build up of deposits on fabrics may also turn yellow in the heat of a dryer. To overcome this problem, you must have soft water obtained from a natural source, by the installation of a mechanical water softener or by addition of chemical water softening agents to the wash. Chemical water softeners such as washing soda, borax or ammonia must be used for both wash and rinse where hard water is used.

Water hardness figures, expressed in grains or parts per million, can be found out from the local municipal water board. You can use this as a yardstick to judge exactly how much interference with the cleaning process can be expected from the water you have at your disposal. Since water hardness varies in different parts of the country and also in the same place at different times, you will have to use some degree of experimentation to arrive at the minimum quantity of soap you will require for an average load of clothes you wash.

It is, of course, normal for soap to form suds. The quantity of suds will depend on the amount of product used, the amount of hardness of the water, the kind and amount of dirt on the clothes, the volume of clothes and so on. Unless there is enough soap present to tie up the minerals which cause water hardness, and to remove and suspend the dirt, there will be no suds. Soap suds are an accurate – and very important – gauge of a soap's ability to clean. Further, a soap sud's head of about 2 inches *must be* maintained all through the wash part of the washer's cycle; once a soap sud's head breaks down, cleaning has ceased and dirt is being redeposited on the clothes.

You can get 7 lb bags of pure soap flakes from A. W. Gamage Ltd., Holborn, London EC1, tel: 01-405 8484, by mail order or direct from the store.

Washing-up liquids

These are also synthetic detergents and there are no real alternatives, but you can cut down on the amount you use. According to WHICH? magazine Fairy Liquid is about the best buy. It is also the most concentrated brand and you can try experimenting to see how little you need to use. You can probably cut use by 50 per cent if you dilute it to half water, half detergent, and give the same number of squeezes.

6. ALL POWER POLLUTES

6 ALL POWER POLLUTES

Each of the major forms of power generation does its own kind of harm to the environment. Fossil fuels – coal and oil – produce smoke and sulphur dioxide at worst; even under ideal conditions they convert oxygen to carbon dioxide.

Hydro-electric power requires dams that cover up land, spoil wild rivers, increase water loss by evaporation, and eventually produce valleys full of silt. Nuclear power stations produce thermal and radioactive pollution and introduce the probability of other disasters. Yet a perpetually expanding energy output is accepted as inevitable without considering the increased pollution this would involve.

WHY BE CONCERNED ABOUT ENERGY

Throughout the one hundred and seventy years since Thomas Malthus proposed that the geometric growth of the world's population was bound, someday, to outstrip the capacity of the Earth to feed that population, the debate over his proposition has raged. Although the question of how many people the world can feed is far from resolved, the general consensus seems to be that constraints other than lack of food will probably limit the population first, at least in many parts of the world. This theory is certainly being borne out in most industrial countries. It isn't hunger so much as the deterioration of our air and water, and the rapid consumption of mineral resources that has indicated to us that we are bumping up against some of those Malthusian limits.

The reaction of some people has been to attribute all of

our environmental ills to overpopulation, yet the fact is that most of the problems are growing much faster than our population is. There is a growing awareness that the problems are in large part due to our standard of living and the expanding rate of consumption this involves. The purpose of this chapter is to illustrate the connexion between our increased standard of living and pollution, by examining the energy-consumption problem.

Why concentrate on energy? Because here the connexion is especially clear. Many of the biggest polluters are really industries which sell energy – in the form of gas, petrol, oil, electricity, and coal.

Higher levels of power consumption have also been one of the clearest indicators of increased living standards. Unfortunately high living standards have also expressed themselves in an increase in environmental problems related to energy production. Among these are:

- More oil spills like the *Torrey Canyon*.
- More black lung disease and gas accidents for miners.
- More sulphur dioxide in the air from fossil-fuel plants.
- More radioactive wastes to dispose of.
- More hazards from nuclear power plants.
- More pump-storage facilities for peak power supply.
- More unsightly distribution lines and an increase in the 50,000 pylons already in England and Wales.
- More waste heat to thermally pollute our rivers and estuaries.
- More power stations which take up more land.

This is what production of power has meant in the past, but what are the chances of providing customers with non-polluting energy in the future? It is true that sulphur can be extracted from fuels before they are burned, and from waste gases before they are emitted. The risk of a blow-out or a spill can be reduced. Distribution lines can be placed underground, at much greater cost. Open-cast coal mines and plant sites can be reclaimed. However, while risks can be minimized, they can never be eliminated. As long as more oil wells must be drilled and more oil must be moved on the seas, more oil will be spilled. Furthermore, the energy industry has met increased demand by scaling up its operations and by adopting new technologies such as nuclear power. Thus the consequences of a miscalculation are becoming more disastrous.

In addition, there will continue to be competition for land and water resources. Hydro-electric potential is realized at the cost of flooded valleys and free-flowing rivers. Extraction of fuel will continue to reduce land values, and destroy scenic beauty. Thermal power plants, either fossil-fuel or nuclear, will continue to produce waste heat and their use of water for cooling is expected to increase. Burning fuels, too, add to the burden of carbon dioxide in the atmosphere.

Many consider nuclear power to be the solution to the disadvantages of other energy sources. At the moment nuclear power plants generate 29,000 million kilowatt-hours (KWh) of the 178,000 million KWh Britain produces but growth in nuclear capacity has lagged behind predictions because of technical problems and the increased costs of capital equipment.

There have been other advances in the technology of energy production; widespread use of these lies just over the horizon. The new nuclear fast breeder reactors use radio-active 'waste' called plutonium from thermal nuclear power plants. At Dounreay there is such an experimental plant; these generators are expected to be important for conservation because uranium, like most other fuels, is a limited resource. The advantage of the fast breeder reactor is that it can 'breed' at least as much fuel as it consumes, thus extracting infinitely more of the potential energy from natural uranium.

Less dramatic advances such as magneto-hydrodynamics

(MHD) and electro-gasdynamics (EGD) will increase the efficiency of the conversion of other forms of energy to electricity.

Thermo-electric generators, solar batteries and fuel cells are available now, but their high cost is too high. Tidal and wind energy are possibilities in certain areas but only fuel cells are likely to become economically competitive with present methods of power generation.

Despite these technical advances, per capita increase in energy consumption will involve a comparable detrimental effect on the environment until less demanding energy production systems are introduced. With nuclear power there is still the danger of accident and the problem of nuclear waste disposal, as well as thermal water pollution. We still use the limited supplies of fossil fuel at a wasteful rate with inefficient energy conversion. Hydro-electricity, although of minor importance in Britain, is unlikely to be welcome if further expansion is considered.

With competitive advertising and other incentives, different utilities are constantly urging the consumer to use more power by buying central heating, electric gadgets and other appliances.

As with other forms of consumption much of the energy we consume is unnecessary or, at the very least, wasteful. The environmentally concerned consumer should try to minimize his use of power.

■ Transportation accounts for a significant amount of energy consumption. So the less you use your car, the better.

■ You can reduce the amount of energy you use in heating, cooling, lighting, and running the appliances in your home.

■ You can reduce your consumption of products that require a lot of energy in their manufacture. For example, aluminium is made by a process that uses about 10 kilowatt-hours of energy per pound just to recover the free metal from the ore.

■ Peak power demand comes at different times of the

day and different seasons of the year. Since your local Electricity Board must have enough capacity to meet peak demand with a little to spare, anything you can do to lower that peak demand will help reduce the need to build pump storage facilities and other installations which deal with peak period power.

Pollution, too, tends to be worst at peak power times. Cutting back on your consumption of energy is a very good way to take action against a whole flock of environmental ills. Such action has the additional advantage of saving you money which you can then spend on more ecologically sound products or pastimes.

COMPARING ENERGY CONSUMPTION

You can spend a very enlightening time doing some sums on the amount of energy used by different appliances in your home.

The following Table (6) provides you with a means of converting various fuels into standard British Thermal Units (BTU), so that you can compare the energy consumption of appliances that use different energy sources.

Table 6. Energy equivalents.

1 Therm	=	100,000 BTU
1 KWh (100% conversion)	=	3,413 BTU
1 lb Propane Gas	=	21,650 BTU
1 cu ft Propane Gas	=	2,500 BTU
1 lb Butane Gas	=	21,500 BTU
1 cu ft Butane Gas	=	3,200 BTU
1 cu ft Natural Gas	=	1,050 BTU
1 gal Domestic Fuel Oil	=	132,900–144,300 BTU
1 gal petrol	=	126,000 BTU
1 lb bituminous coal	=	13,100 BTU

Although these energy equivalents are intended to help you figure *relative* costs, it may help to remember that Therms and British Thermal Units are both units of heat. A Therm is defined as the amount of heat which is needed to raise one gram of water one degree Centigrade. A BTU is the amount needed to raise one pound of water one degree Fahrenheit. To convert electric energy use in KWh to the BTU equivalent of the fuel used to generate it, you should correct for the efficiency of the conversion. Thus, if you want to compare a coal-fired boiler with an electric heater you should really take into account the amount of coal used in the generation of the electricity in the first place. The efficiency with which coal is converted to electrical energy is about 28 per cent in this country. You will find that the direct use of electricity for heating is a very expensive way of using fossil-fuel resources. It has obvious advantages for lighting but direct use of gas provides the same convenience of supply.

With this Table and the following Table (7) of power consumption of electric appliances you should be able to calculate over a period of a year which items use the most power relative to their usefulness, cost, or convenience.

These figures are based on the national averages for the USA. In Britain we are not so free with our use of appliances but you can try and time yourself and work out a weekly average.

Table 7. Estimated power consumption of electric appliances

Appliance	Average Wattage	Estimated Use	Estimated KWh Consumed Annually
Coffee maker	894	20 min/day	106
Dishwasher	1,201	50 min/day	363
Food mixer	127	17 min/day	13
Hot plate	1,257	12 min/day	90
Cooker	12,207	16 min/day	1,175
Roaster	1,333	25 min/day	205
Toaster	1,146	5·6 min/day	39
Refrigerator (12 cu ft)	241	34% of the time	728
Clothes Dryer	4,856	34 min/day	993
Iron (hand)	1,008	23 min/day	144
Washing Machine (automatic)	512	33 min/day	103
Washing Machine (non-automatic)	286	44 min/day	76
Electric blanket	177	2·3 hours/day	147
Fan	370	2·2 hours/day	291
Hair Dryer	381	42 min/week	14
Heater (radiant)	1,322	22 min/day	176
Shaver	14	210 min/day	18
Sun lamp	279	66 min/week	16
Toothbrush	7	117 min/day	5
Water Heater (standard)	2,475	4·7 hours/day	4,219
Water Heater (quick recovery)	4,474	2·9 hours/day	4,811
Radio	71	3·3 hours/day	86
Television (black & white)	237	4·2 hours/day	362
Television (colour)	332	4·1 hours/day	502
Clock	2	100% of the time	17
Sewing Machine	75	2·8 hours/week	11
Vacuum Cleaner	63¼	84 min/week	46

Source: Edison Electric Institute.

WATCH THE ENERGY FLOW INTO
YOUR HOME

To get something approaching a tangible feeling for the electricity you use, find the electricity meter in your home. The faster its small disc turns, the more energy your home is using. Try to turn everything off, then watch what happens when the refrigerator clicks on or off. Try turning on a light, the television, or the toaster. The meter register gives a reading of how many kilowatt-hours of energy flows into your home.

In a similar way you can watch the cubic feet of gas flow into your home to run the cooker, hot-water heater, or boiler.

ELECTRIC APPLIANCES

There was once a time when clocks were wound by hand, when clothes were hung outside to be dried, disinfected, and freshened by the sun, and when windmill and water-wheel put the elements to work for us. Today almost everything seems to have a plug attached to it. To get an idea of how far this has gone, take an inventory of your own home. Go to the electrical outlets, follow the wires, and see where they lead. Try it.

Attached to the business end of many you will probably find lamps. In the kitchen you are likely to find an electric cooker and a refrigerator, and possibly a dishwasher, toaster, mixer, or percolator. The bathroom may have outlets for an electric shaver, toothbrush, or hair dryer as well. The house may have electric heating for cold weather; elsewhere there maybe a washer, dryer, electric clock, iron, sun lamp, fan, vacuum cleaner, electric blanket, sewing machine, room heater, and power tools. Entertainment would not be possible without a radio, television, or record player. Tomorrow it will be the electric car.

What if you follow the wires to the other end? 201 power stations, 10,329 miles of transmission lines and more than 50,000 pylons.

No one can deny the convenience of electricity but some of our appliances have proved to be a mixed blessing. Consider electronic rock music hitting our ears at 115 decibels, the shattering effect that television has had on our modern life style – on participation sports, the arts, and reading.

SO WHAT CAN THE CONSUMER DO?

The first question always is *do you need it*? Do you really need an electric can-opener, electric hedge trimmer or power lawn mower. *If you have it, do you need to use it so much?* Many of the machines in the home are used far more than they need be. How about trying the following:

■ Don't turn on the dishwasher or the washing machine until you have a full load.

■ If you live in an area where the air is clean, why use a clothes dryer on a sunny day? Hang the clothes outside, and see how fresh they smell when you take them in.

■ Turn off unneeded lights.

■ Don't use a waste disposal unit when you can create a compost pile with the organic rubbish instead.

Can you share it? Not everyone needs to have exclusive ownership of everything. We can see what happens when everyone has a car. What can you arrange to share?

A lawn mower?

A sewing machine?

A washing machine or dryer?

Lighting

No one lights his home with anything but electricity any longer – a good development, everything considered. Gas and oil lamps and candles created a good deal of smoke and were a safety hazard. How many unnecessary lights though, does your family leave on? Each ceiling light uses 75 to several hundred watts of power, each lamp 60 to 200 watts.

One unneeded 100 watt bulb left on all day uses 24 KWh. That is 876 KWh a year. At ½p. per KWh that adds £4·38p to your yearly electrical bill – see how it adds up and the environment, your environment, must absorb the costs that go with those extra 876 KWh.

Here are some of the ways you can reduce your consumption of energy for lighting in the home.

■ Turn off lights when they are not needed.

■ During the day, open the curtains and blinds and use the natural light that is free and non-polluting.

■ Different tasks require different amounts of light. Table 8 indicates recommended minimum levels of illumination. Note that in general lighting levels could be less intense.

■ The colour and finish of walls, ceiling, floors, and furniture control light intensity and texture. Keep this in mind when decorating your home and choosing a work-place.

■ Replaced high-wattage bulbs with lower wattage bulbs where high-intensity light is not needed.

■ Fluorescent lighting is significantly more efficient than normal incandescent lighting – about 62 lumens per watt vs. 14 lumens per watt. Fluorescent bulbs also produce less wasted heat and last seven to ten times as long as incandescent bulbs.

■ Keep your lighting fixtures clean so that you get all the light you should.

Refrigerators

Refrigerators and freezers are very useful for the modern home-keeper. They permit him to buy in quantity and to reduce food spoilage.

Most refrigerators and freezers are run by electric power. That means it takes 3·3 to 8·3 KWh per day to operate. Although the machines have a relatively long life, when they *do* expire they have to go somewhere. Too often they end up as unreclaimed waste metal, posing a hazard of suffocation for playing children who get locked inside.

Table 8. Minimum recommended levels of illumination

Task	Light Intensity (*in foot-candles*)
Reading and writing:	
Handwriting, indistinct print	70
Books, magazines, newspapers	30
Recreation:	
Playing cards, tables, billiards	30
Table tennis	20
Grooming:	50
Kitchen work:	
At sink	70
At work counters	50
Laundering jobs:	
At washer	50
At ironing board	50
Sewing:	
Dark fabrics (fine detail, low contrast)	200
Prolonged periods (light-to-medium fabrics)	100
Occasional (light-coloured fabrics)	50
Handicraft:	
Close work (reading diagrams, fine finishing)	100
Measuring, sawing, assembling	50
General lighting:	
Any area involving a visual task	30
For safety in passage areas	10
Areas used mostly for relaxation, recreation, and conversation	10

Source: 'Planning Your Home Lighting' (No. 138, USA Department of Agriculture).

Cookers

The major choice the buyer must make is between gas and electric cookers.

The inherently lower efficiency of electric power production is largely compensated for by the greater efficiency of the electric heating element and the electric oven. It is estimated that 75 per cent efficiency for the electric element versus 40 per cent for the gas burners is average. Similarly, the electric oven, which is relatively airtight, lets out much less waste heat than the gas oven, which must cycle fresh air through the oven to keep a proper mixture for combustion at the burner. Based on industrial data, total energy consumption for the two appliances is similar (gas cooker at 105 Therms per year $=10·5$ million BTU versus electric cooker at 1,175 KWh per year $= 1,175 \times 10,371 = 12.2$ million BTU).

The gas cooker however may be more convenient for rapid temperature changes. Electric cookers also vary in their efficiency and may be largely a matter of personal choice.

Dishwashers

Washing dishes is one of the most unloved tasks in the home. What are the options you have in dealing with the problem?

Using disposable cups, plates, utensils, and prepared foods is not an environmentally sound alternative. It is expensive and increases the solid waste problem.

Washing dishes by hand permits you to minimize use of water. If you live in an area where clean water is not plentiful, try consciously to conserve water. Don't run the rinse water continuously – try using a separate bowl.

There are several things you can do to diminish the environmental effects of dishwashers if you own one:

■ Use a minimal amount of detergent.

■ Your washer may have a drying cycle. You can conserve power and still have dry dishes by interrupting it partway through this cycle, or you can cut the cycle out entirely and hand-dry the load. The latter is a better way of getting around the problem of spotty glassware than is the use of a further rinse.

■ Use the dishwasher only when you have a full load,

since each cycle uses twelve to sixteen gallons of water. Buy the machine that uses the smallest amount of water.

Food waste disposers

These are usually electrically-operated, grinding, waste disposers fitted below the sink. They are comparatively rare here but in the USA there are 8 million of them.

Their job is to reduce food waste to a slurry which can be flushed into a sewer system. Rubbish handled in this way would contribute 20–25 per cent more organic waste load on to municipal sewage farms. Widespread use of these units would need more treatment facility which would have to be paid for from rates. The units cannot be used with a septic tank. Because of this increased waste load they make on the sewers they have been banned in New York City. They only deal with 10–15 per cent of household refuse and all things considered are environmentally damaging for the community.

Also, as anyone who has used one can tell you, food waste disposers add many decibels to the noise levels of the home. Investigate the alternatives. Even if you have a waste disposer, you don't have to use it.

▪ If you live in a rural or suburban area, you should be able to compost your food waste.

▪ If you live in a city, find out how your rubbish and waste water are handled. If your rubbish goes to a rat-infested dump and your waste water to a secondary and tertiary treatment facility, it might make sense to use a waste disposer.

Washing machines

The job of the washing machine is basically very simple: to agitate the clothes in a washing liquid that frees the dirt, to rinse away the dirty water, and to free the clothes of excess water before their final drying. The range of options is wide – from the scrubbing board to the automatic machine with a spin dryer, to the elaborately 'programmed' machines that automatically vary water temperatures and offer pre-soak cycles and extra rinses. Advanced models would automatically dispense detergent, bleach, and fabric softeners at the proper moment and permit you to vary the water level.

Power consumption is probably less of a problem with washers than is water use and pollution They are all excessive water users. When you shop for a washing machine, look for one that will enable you to limit your use of water. Again, if you don't need one don't buy one. Most urban areas have a local Launderette which is much cheaper to use in the long run.

Table 9. Output of electric appliances, UK, 1969

	Number of appliances
Domestic fridges and freezers	1,101,016
Transistor radios, and Electric gramophone turntables	6,683,000
Television sets	1,902,000
Electric blankets	1,459,000
Cookers (5KWh and over)	651,000
Electric irons	2,112,000
Toasters	313,000
Vacuum cleaners	1,887,000
Washing machines	829,000

Source: Central Statistical Office. Annual Abstract of Statistics No. 107, 1970.

7. TRANSPORT: WHERE IS IT TAKING US?

7 TRANSPORT: WHERE IS IT TAKING US?

THE CAR

The private car and all that goes with it is one of the most dominant influences in our consumer society. The desirability of a flexible private means of transport has been cultivated into a vast industry producing 1,700,000 cars a year, costing the consumer £1,500 million, and employing 507,000 people for their manufacture. There are also large numbers employed in servicing, fuel supply and promotion. (In the USA, where the automobile is a more dominant part of the economy, one out of every seven employees is occupied either directly or indirectly with the motor industry.)

Although the car means a great deal to the national economy and to the individuals who own them there is little doubt that, despite its many conveniences, its vast cost in social, economic and environmental terms is destroying our communities, our land, our resources, our atmosphere and our very lives. It is both a symptom and a cause of a large proportion of the environmental diseases we see around us every day, and it has become one of the most powerful tools of psychological manipulation and consumer enslavement ever devised.

Let's look briefly at some of the real environmental costs of the motor car.

Some social costs

■ In the UK the cost of each road accident in hospital bills, car damage, emergency services, etc., is at least £1,500.

■ Each year there are 7,500 deaths from road accidents,

65,000 serious injuries, and 200,000 minor injuries.

■ The increasing number of cars trying to get into our cities causes nuisance to pedestrians, destroys historic buildings, and clogs the streets for emergency services and delays those who travel by public transport.

■ It's not much fun for the driver either, condemned to focus all his faculties on driving, waiting in congested streets, and straining every nerve in frustration.

■ Car accident claims are clogging up our courts, reducing the effectiveness of our whole system of justice.

■ A large number of people are tied up in the manufacture, promotion, and maintenance of cars. An increasing amount of time is used in policing cars by traffic wardens, and expensive planning schemes are devised to adjust to ever-increasing numbers.

■ Noise from cars and other traffic amounts to 85 per cent of the noise nuisance in urban areas.

Cost in land and space

■ The private car spends most of its time unused. Extensive space must be taken up just to provide a stall for the beast – in fact several stalls; at home, office and shopping centres – and parking space is always paved, rendering it useless for anything else and increasing water run-off.

■ There are already only 65 yards of road for every car in Britain and the proportion is rapidly getting smaller. Yet the average car load is only 1·2 persons. The costs of road construction and maintenance are phenomenal but can best be imagined by comparing them with what could be done with the money. For instance, the Greater London Council's proposed motorway building programme is going to cost £2,000 million and account for the demolition of 20,000 houses. This is five times the total capital expenditure on all eight of London's new towns since 1947, which have provided homes for nearly half a million people and 226 new schools.

■ £3,400 million is to be spent on inter-urban trunk roads

over the next 15–20 years. There are already 206,125 miles of road, and their maintenance and administration cost £238 million in 1968.

■ 23 per cent of the area of London is covered by roads.

■ In terms of space, a transport corridor given over to a road and cars would move only 1/17 the number of people that could be moved in the same space by buses, and only 1/12 the load that trains could carry.

Consider the costs in resources

■ In the USA an incredible 9 million cars are scrapped each year, and in Britain 1,700,000 cars are produced each year and 600,000 scrapped.

■ More than 12 million of these mobile masses of metal in the UK consume approximately 13 million tons of petrol per year.

■ Petroleum fuel resources are limited and world supplies are presently calculated to last approximately 60 years. In one oil-producing country, Venezuela, economically viable sources of oil will be exhausted in 13 years.

■ To build just one motorway interchange 26,000 tons of steel, 250,000 tons of concrete, and 3 million tons of earth movement are required.

■ It wouldn't be so bad if cars were built to last – underbody rust alone is estimated to cost vehicle owners a total of £250 million per year in the UK. Many cars end up on the scrap heap even before the HP instalments have been fully paid. The cost of maintenance during their short lives can often amount to more than was paid for the vehicle in the first place.

Pollution costs

The petrol that is burned in your car engine is a mixture of one hundred or more chemical compounds, most of them hydrocarbons (chemicals consisting basically of different arrangements of carbon and hydrogen atoms). When completely burnt this mixture of hydrocarbons gives heat energy, carbon dioxide and water, but with the internal combustion engine the exhaust gases always contain partially burnt hydrocarbons. Added to this there are also crank-case emissions and evaporation from the carburettor and fuel system.

■ These exhaust fumes now contribute the greatest proportion of gaseous air pollution in cities, no doubt contributing to Britain's unenviable record of the world's highest death rate from bronchitis.

■ Although cars are mobile sources of pollutants, they congregate in busy streets and the gases in turn concentrate at ground level and in basement flats.

■ Exposure to exhaust gases also has an effect on the car drivers themselves. According to the Consumer Council in Denmark, concentration and speed of reaction is lowered by 25 per cent. No wonder we often arrive home from motor trips both tense and exhausted.

Other gases

Carbon monoxide provides the largest proportion of the gases coming out of the exhaust. It is a poisonous gas and in busy streets concentrations can rise to more than three times that which the Ministry of Transport considers is a dangerous level. The UK standard is already twice that allowed in the US. We are lucky that most British cities are windy places and that weather inversions which trap the air, such as that which caused the great London smog of 1952, are relatively rare.

As cars accelerate, the exhaust also contains up to 4 per cent of nitrogen oxides which can damage lungs and cause bronchitis and pneumonia.

Lead in fuel

Tetraethyl lead is probably the best-known petrol additive and is used as a cheap way to increase the octane rating, modifying the rapid combustion rate achieved in modern engines, so enabling car drivers to achieve quicker acceleration at traffic lights.

A quarter to one half of this lead ends up in the air as particles – the part of the exhaust pollution that you can see – which eventually reach your lungs or settle on the ground, or on anything else, such as fruit and vegetables being sold or grown near to the road.

Although the petrol manufacturer who adds the lead, and the Ministry of Transport who lets him do this, both say it is harmless, any amount of highly poisonous substances, such as lead, should be reduced even if mass poisoning has not been the result. The problem with most poisons which are found in low concentrations is that they do *not* kill us outright, but add to the progressive impairment of our faculties, accelerated by every other undesirable form of pollution and source of stress.

There is still some evidence of the direct effects of exhaust lead. In Britain it has been found that low lead exposure slows down the ability of nerve endings to react as rapidly as they should, and in the USA a direct relation has been found between lead settling in residential areas and heart diseases. As with carbon monoxide, lead obviously concentrates in certain areas, such as those near to motorways or in basement flats.

Besides the effects of lead on health, its addition to petrol is a scandalous waste of resources since nearly 40 per cent of the world's lead production is used as fuel additives. In addition, the production and consumption of the ethyl lead causes further waste of resources. In the USA 85 per cent of sodium metal available is used in the production of ethyl lead and about $\frac{3}{4}$ of the bromide production goes into making ethyl dibromide, 90 per cent of which is used to prevent lead deposits in car engines.

In the USA non-leaded petrols have been available for some time and most US manufacturers will design their 1971 cars to operate on non-leaded fuel.

In the UK the Government has been slow to take up this

problem, even though the lead levels in blood among city children have already been found to be abnormally high. The evidence used to support Government complacency is somewhat suspect since it is derived from old records, and most medical research on the subject has been done under the auspices of the lead manufacturers themselves.

Presently the UK Government is considering a ban on lead fuel additives, and both BP and Shell are developing lead-free petrols in response. When they arrive on the market they should be used in preference to leaded varieties.

Other pollutants from cars

Although car exhaust is the main source of gaseous pollution from cars, it is not commonly realized that asbestos from brake-linings, and rubber from tyres, are both cancer-producing agents and are released into the air we breath. The extent of this form of particulate pollution may be imagined just from the £90 million we spend each year on new tyres.

Besides the pollutants that are produced by the car as it is driven along, we must add the pollution caused by the steel, glass and paint that form part of the production of the car in the first place, not forgetting the pollution from the plants which make cement and asphalt for roadways.

ALTERNATIVE ENGINES

Despite its cost the present car engine doesn't even do its job very well. If we didn't have cars and were obliged to devise a transport system to give everyone the opportunity of a flexible means of getting around, then engineers would blink in horror at the inefficiency and wastefulness of the motor car and its internal combustion engine compared with the alternative engines and forms of transport that we already have at our disposal.

Diesel engines

The diesel engine is widely used, especially in lorries and buses. Believe it or not, a properly working diesel actually pollutes less in some respects than your car engine – because the diesel burns hotter, combustion is more complete. This reduces hydrocarbons and carbon monoxide to low levels but tends to increase nitrogen oxides. It is possible to reduce emissions and noise from bus diesels, but for the car, the diesel is not much of an improvement over the petrol-powered internal combustion engine.

Wankel engines

The Wankel engine is a rotary internal combustion engine that has the advantage over the standard reciprocating-piston type, being smaller and more compact. Commercial production of cars with this engine has already taken place in Japan (Toyo Kogyo Co) and in Germany (NSU Co). NSU has produced 10,000 units of its RO-80 full-scale saloons. The Wankel engine, however, is at least as polluting as the normal internal combustion engine, but with exhaust reactor systems it too can be brought up to (currently) acceptable levels.

Away from internal combustion

In the early days of the motor car, steam and electric cars were as common as petrol-powered ones. The internal combustion engine (i.c.e.) became dominant not because it was a significant improvement over other types. In fact, the advantages that led to the investment of larger amounts in i.c.e. research were relatively few. Since that time infinitely more research has gone into the perfection of the i.c.e. than into steam, electric, and other power alternatives, but today, faced with the new challenges posed by air pollution and other problems, we find manufacturers turning back to take a second look at the alternatives. Cars have become such complex machines that it is no wonder that they don't work the way one would like them to. It is time for a fresh look.

A large number of working prototypes of other systems have been built. Many of them have significant advantages over the internal combustion engine – both in terms of emissions, and in economy of operation and maintenance. At the present time, however, none of them have been mass-produced, and only when the economies of mass production come into play will they provide a feasible alternative for the general car buyer.

Unfortunately, the petrol-powered internal combustion engine is today so entrenched that switching to another power system would require an enormous adjustment. The biggest obstacle in the way of better power systems for private and public vehicles is the inertia of the major car producers, especially those in the USA. Innovation is coming from outside the industry though, and with Government help and prodding, new systems should become available. It may be that in 15 or 20 years time the internal combustion engine car will be an oddity.

Electric cars

60,000 electric vehicles are presently in use in England. Many of these are, of course, the familiar milk carts and delivery vans, but electric vehicles can be used for other purposes. For instance, in the US there are about 150,000 golf carts powered by electric storage batteries, and numerous small trucks are in use in warehouses and airports.

For certain purposes, the electric-powered vehicle has an impressive list of advantages. Aside from a small amount of ozone, the car produces no air pollution during operation. It operates quietly, a significant asset when one remembers all the noise coming from i.c.e. powered vehicles. Although the electric car lacks speed and extensive range at present, most city and suburban driving requires neither.

The most commonly mentioned problem regarding large-scale use of electric-powered cars is the vastly increased load this would put on the electric power industry. While cars could not pollute the air directly, the power plants would. This may increase the load on power stations by as much as 40 per cent and would mean exchanging a substantial increase in electric power production for the abolition of automobile air pollution. It is not immediately clear which would be more desirable.

The i.c.e. is only about 15 per cent efficient. Thermodynamically, the highest efficiency possible is 25 per cent to 30 per cent, but this has not been achieved. Part of the reason is that the i.c.e. usually operates at far less than its optimum; idling is, of course, wholly wasteful. The electric car wouldn't lose energy in this way. Assuming generation efficiency of electric power at 35 per cent, and taking into account the losses of energy in the motor (10 per cent), charging the batteries (20 per cent), and transmitting the power (10 per cent), one can calculate that the over-all efficiency of an electric vehicle would be about 23 per cent, varying according to the energy content of the power plant fuel. This is a substantial improvement in efficiency over the i.c.e., and would tend to mean less pollution for this reason, though the nature and site of the pollution would differ.

From an energy-resource point of view, therefore, the electric car might be a good idea. If fuel cells with efficiencies greater than 35 per cent become economically feasible, or if nuclear or fossil-fuel energy can ever be made truly clean, then electrically-driven cars will become the main vehicles of choice.

Coming back to the present, however, one must recognize that fuel cell technology is not ready and that present battery systems are either much heavier than we would want, or too expensive. Working within these limits, a number of prototypes of electric cars have been built. In 1967-8 there was a great flurry of interest in electric cars, but to date no widely acceptable model is on the market.

The word 'acceptable' is the key. Electric cars do not have the performance of the high-powered i.c.e. cars of today, but it is not at all clear that any car should. It depends on what you are looking for, but for most, existing electric vehicles should be acceptable. For that matter, so should any small, low-powered vehicle. In fact, the greatest virtue that electric vehicles should have is that they may enable people to think beyond a framework that demands increasing power and speed.

▪ Ford (UK) have an experimental electric car called the Commuta. It gives a top speed of 45 mph and a range of 40 miles. It is big enough for two adults and two children.

▪ Some time ago Enfield Automotive announced firm production plans for a four-seater electric car directed towards the US market and selling at around £450. So far this vehicle has not appeared on the market. The Enfield has a top speed of 40 mph, a 35-mile range and an eight-hour recharge period.

There are several other cars being developed in the USA, such as that by Electric Fuel Propulsion Inc, of Detroit, which has delivered 42 of its Mars II electric cars, mainly to electric companies. They are capable of speeds up to 70 mph, can cruise at 40 mph for 150 miles, and can be charged to 80 per cent of capacity in 45 minutes. A similar vehicle was demonstrated in New York in December 1969. It can be mass-produced at between £1,500 and £2,000 and costs only 50p for a full charge.

Rankine engines

Rankine engines are external combustion engines that use a working fluid in a closed system to deliver energy that drives a piston or turbine. The working fluid may be steam as in the steam car, hydrogen or helium as in the Sterling engine, or another fluid. Several advantages are given by its advocates. The Rankine vehicle is supposed to be more economical to operate because it has better maintenance and reliability potential. Its acceleration, auxiliary operation, and braking characteristics are superior to those of the i.c.e. Alleged 'problems' in applying Rankine cycle systems to car use have been, or are being, solved. The Rankine cycle engine is as safe as the i.c.e., it consumes no more water, freeze-up can be avoided, and the start-up time is 20 seconds with a cold engine. Paraffin, low-octane petrol, natural gas, oil and even coal can be used to power a Rankine engine.

Working models of steam and other Rankine engine-powered cars have been around for some time, but the motor industry seems to have too much at stake in the i.c.e. for them to become widely accepted.

Gas turbine

The advantage of the gas turbine over steam is primarily because it is mechanically simpler.

Like the Rankine-powered car, the gas turbine has very low emissions, it burns readily available inexpensive fuel, and it has been proven in performance and consumer acceptance. In the early 1960s Chrysler in the USA built 50 turbine cars which tested out quite successfully.

The main problem seems to be the cost of building the turbines and the rate at which they can be turned out. These are problems that could be solved fairly quickly with a little development money. Turbine engines for lorries and buses are scheduled for introduction in the USA in mid-1971, thus prospects for turbines in cars are probably good.

The flywheel car

One of the most fascinating developments recently has been the novel possibility of a car or bus powered either by a rapidly-spinning flywheel, or by a flywheel coupled to another engine.

The principle of the flywheel is the same as that which keeps a child's top spinning. Although the specially-shaped flywheel for use in a car engine requires complicated design considerations, it would operate similarly to the spinning top in that an initial amount of energy, probably from an electric power source, would set it spinning at high speed. The use of this principle of propulsion is well known and has been used in the torpedo since the late 1880s when an initial burst of power set the flywheel spinning and the torpedo cutting through the water to its target without the need for an engine.

The most well-developed experiment has been the use of the flywheel in the 70-seater Oelikon bus which was first introduced in 1953 and has been in use in various countries of Europe and Africa. The flywheel used to be recharged in about 2 minutes from an overhead cable rather like the old trolley buses in London, when the flywheel kept the bus going until the next bus stop. This was rather awkward, though, as the bus had to stop at each bus stop whether or not there were passengers to be collected. With the latest type of super flywheel however, the Oelikon bus could travel the whole route without having to be re-charged.

The main directions of development have been to reduce the weight and increase the speed, thus increasing the capacity of the flywheel to store energy. The future result for the car, according to the development group at John Hopkins University in the USA, would be a lighter car which could travel up to 100 miles without recharging, with a saving of 70 per cent of the fuel power presently used in the average internal combustion engine car. Maintenance and other costs would be reduced because it is simpler and would have fewer parts.

The main saving for the city bus would be in fuel costs. The bus could be recharged at night when the load on the electricity power stations is at a minimum. No further increase in power station plants would be needed and engine noise would be considerably reduced. The amount of stored power needed by a bus would mean a more advanced flywheel which may not become available for another decade. Nevertheless, its potential use in smaller forms of transport or for auxiliary power in underground trains and lorries looks promising.

With the development of higher flywheel speeds the safety factor must be considered. The shattering of a flywheel travelling at high speeds presents some hazard, but present research shows possible ways of reducing the danger. The flywheel, when placed horizontally, will in any case add something to the stability of moving vehicles.

Hybrid vehicles

The present i.c.e. car is in fact a hybrid to the extent that it has a battery to start the engine. It was the self-starter that gave the earlier i.c.e. a critical advantage over the steam cars anyway.

More development of hybrid engined vehicles could overcome the disadvantages of some of the commonly-mentioned alternatives to the present i.c.e. For instance, a battery-powered vehicle, equipped with an i.c.e. or an external combustion engine (e.c.e.) power plant which keeps the batteries charged, could overcome the range limitation that is imposed by the limited energy capacity of batteries. In such a system, the engine can be operated at a constant output that is near its highest efficiency and lowest emissions' level. The Sterling hybrid is such a car.

It seems unlikely that any of the possible alternatives will achieve the dominance that the i.c.e. has achieved, and this is certain to be undesirable anyway. However, in the future it is to be hoped that more sense will prevail in the use of different engines and various combinations of types for the wide variety of transport needs.

Your next car

If you really need to renew your car then you should start thinking about some of the alternatives which reduce the car's environmental impact.

It we are to believe the experts, the external combustion engine (Rankine or gas turbine) offers the best choice for meeting the strict emission standards that we will need later in this decade and in the 1980s. Exhaust and emissions will have to be lowered to keep pollution levels from creeping back up as the number of cars increases. Putting abatement devices on the ends of exhaust pipes is only a short term answer anyway. Cars could also be much lighter and more efficient than they are at present.

When you buy a car, look at what you are buying – not in the advertiser's terms but in your own. Until the car ceases to be a status symbol (an idea carefully nurtured by car manufacturers' advertising), people will continue to buy much bigger and more powerful cars than they need or want. The more 'car' you buy, the more you pollute. Keep some of the following in mind:

■ Smaller cars pollute less than large ones. They have smaller engines which get better mileage, and when the car is ready to be scrapped there is less car to be disposed of.

■ A car that doesn't weigh much doesn't need power steering and power brakes. These add to the costs of running a large car.

■ The less fuel your car burns per mile of operation, the less fuel that has to be drilled out and transported. Regardless of the other pollutants, less fossil-fuel consumption means less carbon dioxide in the atmosphere.

■ Most cars are vastly over-powered. There is absolutely no need for anything but a racing car to do 100 miles an hour.

■ Small cars cost less.

■ The low-powered cars use lower-octane petrol which is likely to contain less lead.

■ Cars with fuel-injection systems (VW, Porsche, Volvo, Mercedes and Triumph) are better at feeding the proper mixture of petrol and air to each cylinder than cars with carburettors.

■ Keep on the lookout for cars with power that is inherently less polluting than today's internal combustion engines.

■ Gadgets such as power windows, power antennae, power seats, and others add to the amount of energy your motor must use. In addition, the small motors that run these power devices are usually too hard to salvage when the car is demolished for scrap. The copper in the electric motors contaminates the scrap and reduces the value of the car hulk.

■ Some low-powered cars and motor bikes have a two-cycle engine that uses a petrol-oil mixture for fuel. These tend to have visibly high particulate and hydrocarbon emissions.

Your present car

There are a number of ways you can act now to keep your car's contribution to air pollution down.

■ Drive rationally. Quick starts and high speeds drastically increase petrol consumption and pollution. Fuel consumption and tyre wear are 50 per cent higher at speeds of 70–80 mph than at 50. Don't let your engine idle if you can avoid it. Professional drivers on Economy Runs manage to cut petrol consumption markedly by using these techniques.

■ Keep your car in good repair. A well-tuned car (every

6,000 miles) will emit far less pollution. A dead sparkplug can increase emissions.

■ Watch out for petrol leaks. Hydrocarbons that escape from a leaky tank or carburettor are just as harmful as those that come out of the exhaust pipe.

Your car's tyres

When you buy a tyre, you buy a lot of pollution. This is true of almost any manufactured product. Drive in such a way that they will last. Avoid screeching starts and stops. Drive at moderate speeds, for tyre wear is much greater at high speeds. Some tread designs are quieter than others. If you can find a way to determine which types are less noisy, buy that kind.

Worn-out tyres can be put to use. They have been chained together and sunk to the bottom of the ocean to provide anchor points for artificial reefs, and they have been 'chewed up' and used as an ingredient in asphalt. Tyres can also be converted back into liquid oil, natural gas, and solid residues which may have commercial uses.

YOUR TRANSPORT STRATEGY

Because transport consumes such a large share of the resources we spend, both natural and financial, and because it
is such a large contributor to the environmental and social
ills that plague modern society, we should put some thought
into devising a personal transportation strategy that will
work towards a better system. We are no longer free to take
our cars, roads, and planes so much for granted.

In the cities

The first step should be to get an idea of what a desirable
system might mean. To a great extent, we already know
where we should be heading. In terms of efficiency and minimizing pollution, public mass transport is far better than our
present reliance on the private car for urban areas.

The fuel consumption and exhaust emissions can be calculated for different forms of transport, but this is a complex thing to do especially as it has to relate among other
factors, to different numbers of passengers, the road space
each vehicle takes up, and the amount and type of pollution
and waste of resources it causes.

On the basis of pollution and fuel consumption alone,
however, trends do emerge. The car, even when fully loaded
(which it seldom is), is least favourable. Trains and buses
pollute the least. Public transport vehicles also spend a
much larger proportion of their time in service, and generally need only one parking place. While they may not deliver you to the doorstep of your final destination, neither do

they make you walk long distances just because parking spaces are scarce.

Support schemes to prevent cars from entering city centres. Many examples exist where traffic has been restricted from a city centre. This has occurred in Norwich where the old city centre is pleasant to shop in once again, and local trade has increased. Cars do not have to be banned completely, but in areas such as Pimlico in London, through traffic is made impossible by a maze of narrowed-streets and dead-ends. These schemes can be achieved by determined public pressure – and this is what is needed in many cases though it took five years for the GLC to finally decide to restrict traffic in Carnaby Street.

In the suburbs

Urban sprawl is very much tied up with the transportation problem.

Although urban sprawl makes public transport difficult, it should not cause it to be phased out altogether. A network of public transportation corridors could connect with parts of the city, supplemented by a finer network of smaller carriers to service the residential areas. Some experiments are underway with 'dial-a-bus' systems using small 10-passenger vehicles to provide the ultimate flexibility for such a residential service.

Birmingham has experimented with a 'park and ride' system for out-of-town shoppers. Parking spaces are reserved on the outskirts of the city, and free public transport is available into the city shopping centre for the drivers.

The relative costs

What are the relative costs of public transport versus the private car? Taking a total view, it is clear that any system that uses less capital equipment to move more people at a greater operating efficiency must be less expensive. From a personal point of view the greater economy of public transport may not be apparent, but think about the following:

You already subsidize public transport with your fares, and to a significant extent with your rates and taxes. You pay for car expenses too. You invest a large sum to buy a car, and an additional sum to maintain it and to insure it.

In addition, there are the hidden costs of the taxes spent for increasing the capacity of the road system, and for the storm sewer systems that must handle the extra water run-off, and of the taxes not collected because untaxable roads have displaced rate-producing urban property. There is also the added burden of pollution from greater emissions and from more fuel extraction and transport.

If you contribute so much already to subsidize public transport, why not use it more often?

Between cities

As in the city, you have the option to take either your car or public transport when you travel between cities. The fact remains that the car is still a relatively inefficient and expensive way to move people. Rail transport and buses are much to be preferred; and it seems hard to understand the necessity for air travel in a small country like Britain, especially where inter-city train services are cheaper and probably quicker in the long run.

Over long distances, and especially overseas and between countries, speed becomes important. The fast pace of modern living tends to demand air travel, despite its greater price. Unless something can be done about our frantic life style, air travel is unlikely to lose much of its business to less environmentally harmful modes of transportation.

The trend, though, still seems to be towards larger and faster planes. The Boeing 747 moves more people with greater efficiency and less noise, whilst the Concorde would move fewer people with lower efficiency and much greater noise. Just to save a few businessmen a couple of hours, literally millions will be exposed to the sonic bang each time the plane flies. The effects on climate are not known, but they are potentially catastrophic. The enormous production cost to the taxpayer does not make much sense either, and air transport companies are beginning to wonder whether the Concorde will be economic in service.

The trouble too with passenger air transport is that it usually operates at only half capacity or less, even when worked out on a seasonal basis. The financial difficulties of most airlines might force them into a more rational arrangement of passenger services, thus increasing the number of passengers per trip.

For more leisurely air travel and for freight, new developments in airships seem promising. Safe, silent airships can be built to travel at speeds of 100 mph and carry more than 400 passengers. Germany and Japan have already built prototypes which could be powered by nuclear engines when these are safer, or even by auxiliary power from solar energy cells.

Air shuttles, especially helicopter taxis, have come into service but tend to be devices for getting round the failure of ground systems to do the job more efficiently. A full helicopter uses about 26 times as much fuel per passenger as a full train and is much noisier.

Integrated transport

You daily face a series of transport choices. Each time you make one, you have a chance to act for or against your own long term good and that of our society. There are things you can do today that may be as minor as buying a smaller car or taking a bus when normally you could have used your car. Buy a bicycle or walk more. Each act contributes. Get in the habit and encourage others to do the same and the impact will be significant. When a major decision does arise, apply the same criteria. Be willing to try something new. If you have always taken a plane, try an overnight train sleeper. When the holidays come, explore places nearer home.

It will take patience and effort to put up with some inconvenience as we change over to more rational transport strategies. This is part of the conversion process that seems inevitable anyway, so be prepared for it by learning to use a variety of transport opportunities. You may find that the 'more convenient' forms of getting around are not so convenient after all. You can channel some of your inevitable frustration into constructive actions. Let transport authorities know when their system hasn't worked as it should. Join the many pressure groups working for a saner transport policy.

When significant numbers of people begin to act in this way, the impact will be felt. Not everyone has to stop using a product or service to make it economically unfeasible. Conversely, a small but significant increase in patronage can greatly benefit something good.

But the question we must really ask is whether the car, as a flexible, universal and private means of transport is possible even in the near future. At the present rate of car ownership the costs to the individual and the community are rapidly outweighing the benefits. The whole community is probably already paying a tremendous price for the dubious convenience of less than half the population. While the motor industry and highway complexes have mushroomed we have allowed our public transport system to decay, progressively immobilizing those who already suffer most – the poor, the young, the elderly, and the women who have to do most of the fetching and carrying.

The further ideas that follow will hopefully be valuable for those who want to move away from high-cost, polluting transport, to more efficient methods that preserve a little more sanity and possibly a pleasanter, more inhabitable world.

Cars – further ways to help

So far, this chapter on transportation has concentrated on two topics – the choice among various modes of travel, and the costs and operation of the motor car. In so doing, we have covered many of the major transportation decisions most of us face, but there are more ways that you can make a contribution to environmental improvement.

Car pools and offering lifts

Surveys have shown that the average load in the private car is in the range of 1·2 to 1·5 passengers in a vehicle made to hold between 4 and 6 comfortably. Clearly, one of the ways to reduce pollution and fuel consumption is to fill up the cars that will inevitably be on the road. Then we wouldn't need as many cars to carry the same number of people.

The car pool is a good way of accomplishing this. If you have no choice but to drive to work and you know others who live nearby with whom you can make such an arrangement, do so. In this way you can cut down on operating expenses, help to alleviate traffic congestion, and free the car you leave at home for more active service. It might make it possible for you to get along comfortably with one less car in the household if you already have more than one.

Car pooling on a large scale has been shown to be effective in the USA. A San Francisco radio station launched a one-day car pool experiment that reduced the morning traffic load across the Golden Gate Bridge by about 6 per cent. In New York City a phone call can put you in touch with a computer which will tell you the name of a person with whom you can take a lift or form a regular car pool. Many large firms also arrange car pools.

But you don't have to be part of an organized car pool to share the space in your car.

■ The next time you drive to a meeting offer a lift to someone, or ask for a lift from a friend.

■ Make your next shopping trip by car with a friend.

■ If you are going to take a long trip by car and have space for a passenger, find one. Check with friends in advance of departure, or look at notices on college bulletin boards.

■ Unless you are really worried about it, don't be afraid

to offer a lift to a stranger. Hitch-hiking is a common, friendly way to meet interesting people and young foreign visitors.

How about a bicycle?

Consider the advantages that the bicycle has to offer – low cost, no pollution, and convenient to park.

◾ For under £25 you can get a new bicycle fitted with enough trimmings to make it practical for going shopping and carrying a small child. (A second-hand bicycle can be found for much less.) The cheapest car costs about thirty times that.

◾ A bicycle is also inexpensive to operate, maintain and insure.

◾ Bicycles are quieter than any form of motorized transport, produce no pollution, and use up no fuel.

◾ A bicycle takes up about 1/30 of the parking space of a car.

◾ In city traffic today, the bicycle is often faster than a car or bus.

◾ Bicycles give the rider the sort of healthy exercise that many of us need.

◾ Riding a bicycle makes it possible to get a better appreciation of a beautiful day, or a pleasant ride through a park.

It cannot be disputed that riding a bicycle also gives you a better appreciation of a rainy day and the foul exhaust from polluting vehicles that share the road with you. It is not without its drawbacks. Yet even within our foulest cities numerous souls rely on bicycles and enjoy them.

◾ Even if you don't use a bicycle every day of the year you should have one for times when you can make use of it. Many of the short trips you take each day – for a newspaper, to visit a neighbour, to pick up an item or two at the grocer – could be done by bicycle. Even major shopping can be done by bicycle if the store has a delivery service.

◾ And when it is time for a day out, put the family on

bicycles instead of packing them into a car. If you have to travel some distance to find nice riding, take the bicycles along and park the car while you enjoy your ride.

■ You can also put bicycles on trains when you are off on holiday or away for the weekend.

■ The Cyclists' Touring Club at Cotterell House, 69 Meadrow, Godalming, Surrey, is well worth joining if you become a cyclist. It can provide good insurance cover and legal advice in case of accidents, besides offering numerous other benefits.

Walk!

The most natural form of locomotion. Reliable and totally non-polluting, it offers convenience – no parking, no cost. Invigorating, it promotes health and gives you the chance to think.

8. WASTED WEALTH

8   WASTED WEALTH

One of the major products of the UK economy is rubbish. About 16 million tons of it every year.

Much of it consists of material such as glass, paper, rags, and metals, all of which can be recovered. Most of these useful materials, if they remain unrecovered, constitute a vast and growing form of wasted wealth. We must begin to consider rubbish not as an embarrassment but as a resource.

In fact we must also stop thinking of ourselves as consumers, but as users of raw materials. There are probably few things we really 'consume' beyond food and energy, and even this is questionable since all we are doing is transforming one form of energy into another. As we digest food we convert it into heat energy, energy for movement, etc, and it eventually forms part of the global energy budget constantly replenished by the sun. The same goes for plants which are able to store energy until we, or other animals, can use it in the form of food, or until it may become fossilized, as in coal deposits, and be released millions of years later when we burn coal in the grate.

Many of the minerals we use come from plant or animal sources, such as wood or animal fats. They are constantly recycled when we return them to the earth. This system is renewed as seeds germinate and as animals are born, and the mineral resources tend to continue indefinitely if the organic cycles remain unbroken.

The minerals we extract from the earth as ores, such as metals, asbestos, etc., are used by us to make a variety of products. After a period of use the article gets thrown away, or as the article wears out, particles of it enter the atmosphere and eventually settle on the ground. Thus, even durable materials eventually return to the earth. The trouble is that the time they take to convert back to ores and concentrate in certain areas is very, very slow. Coal takes 300 million years to form and other useful minerals may take much longer to accumulate into a readily available form. Thus, supplies of metals, other minerals and fossil fuels, can for practical purposes be considered as non-renewable.

Minerals such as aluminium are so plentiful that their availability is unlikely to become a problem. Others, such as copper and nickel, are used in such quantity that recovery could be relatively easily organized. However, important minerals, such as lead, tin, platinum, and tungsten, occur in much smaller quantities and at the present rate of consumption are likely to last only for the next 20–30 years. We will have great difficulty in finding substitutes for these. Yet compounds of these rarer metals, such as mercury, are poured into rivers and seas at an incredible rate.

The constraints on the continued supply of such materials are many. Obviously a mineral which is naturally rare will be difficult to recover if it is distributed to the environment again in waste water. It may be used in such small quantities that it is difficult and uneconomic to recover.

Much more re-use and recycling of materials must be considered for consumer products, even if they are made from renewable resources. Obviously a great deal is up to industry, especially where the waste comes directly from the production process, but more recovery could take place from household refuse. At the other end of the scale, the rate of consumption and the increased trend towards disposability and rapid obsolescence must be curbed if the present world population is to continue with the limited resources the Earth can provide.

HOUSEHOLD REFUSE

Household refuse accounts for a considerable amount of the total solid wastes produced in this country, and our local authorities spend about £80 million on its collection and disposal – which works out at about 3p per person per week. Unsuitable disposal of waste is an important cause of environmental deterioration, but it is only at the source that most individuals can help. Improvement to local waste management, though, would receive quite a boost if individuals gave it a greater priority when they considered local issues. Much of the continued difficulty, as with water and sewage treatment, is due to the indifferent attitudes of the public who treat waste collection as more of a joke than a necessity. Even a realization of the extent of the amounts involved, brought home to householders by recent strikes, has not aroused much curiosity as to how it is disposed of, or how it can be reduced.

If you think about the contents of your dustbin for a moment (and too few people do) you will quickly realize the incredible range of stuff that goes into it – not only tea-leaves, paper, and ashes, but old kitchen utensils, glass and crockery, and also larger items such as old toys and furniture. Out of this mixture we can find two basic categories – organic waste, such as tea-leaves and cardboard, and inorganic waste, such as crockery and metals. A further category is bulky refuse, which usually means old furniture and other junk that is too big to go inside the dustbin; this accounts for about 6 per cent of the total volume.

The total amount of solid refuse grows every year, and it is estimated that its volume will double in the next twenty years. Yet many towns have already used up all the convenient holes and pits available for dumping, and the changing nature of the refuse is causing technical and other problems for the incinerators and pulverizers that are used to treat it.

Some of the more obvious items which share an increasing proportion of changing household waste are plastic and paper packaging and glass bottles, all of which are the result of more pre-packed foods and over-packaging for advertising and visual appeal. The growing change to oil, gas, and electric heating has meant a reduction in ash and cinder content of household refuse. The density of refuse has also changed. The larger number of disposable containers and the reduction in ashes and cinders has meant that the ratio of volume to weight has increased, and the same lorry load takes less weight of waste than it used to.

WHAT YOU CAN DO TO RECLAIM

Separation

The first rule for the would-be reclaimer is to find a way of separating the waste. At the moment we throw everything into the same bin but most types of recoverable materials are made useless if mixed with everything else, and manual sorting afterwards is too costly. Newspapers are easy to put on one side and can be tied together with string; other items can be stored in bins or bags if you have a garden or suitable space. Often the rag-and-bone merchant will be pleased to take away bulkier stuff if the dustmen aren't.

In the municipal treatment plant, separation of refuse may occur manually or mechanically with magnetic extraction of ferrous metal. The waste can also be composted after separation or, if incinerated, it may generate heat for the local community, and the residue can also be used. Each of the different treatment processes have their advantages but all are preferable to unsightly open dumps which is where most of our rubbish ends up. Burning and composting return waste to the natural cycle quickly, whereas compaction and dumping don't.

Paper

Most of the paper used in Britain comes from someone else's forest, especially those of Canada and Scandinavia. Since it is a major import item, companies in the British Waste Paper Association make a significant contribution to our balance of payments by the collection, processing and return of $1\frac{1}{2}$ million tons of scrap paper to the manufacturers every year, making a saving of £66 million on our import bill.

Dealers have almost reached the limit in terms of the supply available from industry so any further development of the market must look towards domestic sources. Some local authorities encourage people to separate newspapers and rags and arrange for its collection – does yours? – if not, encourage them to do so. Even though the mixture of magazines and boxes, etc, that comes out of a household can only provide low quality waste, it can add to a local authority's income and offset increased costs of disposal.

Most household paper products can be recycled. The easiest to handle is generally newsprint, in part because there is so much of it. A 40-inch stack of newspapers, folded to half-page size as you buy them, weighs 100 pounds. Since a ton of newsprint represents pulp from about 17 trees, recycling a stack of newspapers about 45 inches high saves almost one tree. Recycling a ton of newsprint also eliminates a major portion of the pollution associated with producing new pulp. For the sulphite pulping process, this pollution includes 275 pounds of sulphur, 350 pounds of limestone, 60,000 gallons of water, 9,000 pounds of steam, and 225 kilowatt-hours of electricity, per ton of unbleached pulp.

The price for used newsprint averages about £4·50– £5·50 per ton at the local town agent, and £10·00 per ton direct to the mills in quantities of 5–8 tons. Most of the re-used newsprint goes to make cheap cardboard, but some is made into fresh newspaper. Some newspapers, especially local ones, might be encouraged to start a collection campaign.

Corrugated cardboard also has a ready market. Check with the waste paper dealers in your area. You may be able to sell magazines and even mixed paper if it is not coated and is free of plastics.

Glass

Glass has a ready market for recycling because the crushed glass cullet can be used in glass manufacture to speed up the melting of the virgin silica. To be used for this purpose the cullet must be clean. Thus, when saving glass for recycling, you should rinse out the container, soak off any paper labels, and remove any metal such as the lid or the ring of metal around the top, left by twist-off bottle caps. Separate the bottles by colour. You can reduce the amount of storage space required by breaking the bottles.

Although glass reclamation is praiseworthy, as with all waste materials the best policy for you to follow is still one which minimizes use of all materials whether recyclable or not. The fact that it is recyclable should not be used to justify increased consumption.

Since bottles only have to be washed to be useful again the replacement of soft-drink and milk bottles by non-returnable ones or other plastic containers is to be deplored. A returnable soft-drink bottle used to make about 50 round trips and milk bottles last about 14 rounds on the average.

In one year, 1969, growth of non-returnable bottles has increased from 180 million bottles to 290 million for soft-drinks, and beer bottle sales rose from 20 million to 60 million units.

Beer, soft-drinks, and milk hold the largest share of returnable bottles. Milk will continue to be sold in returnable glass bottles for marketing reasons, but the Glass Manufacturers' Federation estimate that non-returnable soft-drink bottles should reach 350 million by the end of 1970, and 450 million by 1972, and for beer the figures will be 100 million and 250 million respectively.

The soft-drink and beer manufacturer avoids the cost of collection, washing, and transit damage, but everyone has to pay the environmental cost. This phenomenal increase in non-returnable bottles means that the consumer will also be paying more not only for the container but for its disposal as well – through rates. On a broader level we also have to pay in wasted fuel, water, and raw materials for the bottles thrown away which could all be re-used and eventually recycled.

■ Avoid non-returnable bottles, when you possibly can. Return the non-returnable and tell the supermarket or store manager why. You might set up local collection centres for glass at the pub or school. A similar campaign in the USA has forced Coca-Cola to reverse its policy on non-returnables and to set up glass collection centres.

Metals

There is usually a ready market for non-ferrous metals such as copper, lead, zinc, and aluminium. You can read the prices per ton listed each day in the *Financial Times*. Dealers buy at just under this fixed price and sell at just over it. The metal you are likely to accumulate around the home is largely in the form of cans, primarily 'tin' and aluminium. The tin cans are actually steel, and unfortunately the tin coating and lead solder so contaminate the steel that its scrap value is reduced – but in some areas there is still a market. If de-tinning plants were opened, this situation might change.

Beer and soft-drink cans are usually made from steel or aluminium, sometimes steel with an aluminium pull-top lid. Both types have been recycled successfully in the USA. Unfortunately, in this country the economic incentive to collect cans is lacking as well as the fact that our per capita consumption of these items may not be sufficiently great to warrant any special reclamation programmes.

If reclamation of aluminium from pots and pans and cans could be arranged, it would be doubly important, since the manufacture of this metal uses about 10 kilowatt-hours of electric power per pound. Re-melting used metal is much less expensive in terms of energy and consumption. Also, aluminium cans have the property of being almost indestructible when they are discarded as litter. Unlike steel cans, they don't rust. Thus, discarded aluminium becomes a permanent nuisance.

Half of the 26 million tons of crude steel produced in 1969 was processed scrap. Most of this metal is collected by special scrap merchants but many local authorities make little attempt to salvage metals on an organized basis and it is estimated that about £7 million worth is lost each year from domestic refuse by tipping and dumping into pits.

Cloth

Usable or repairable clothing should be sold or given away. Don't destroy good cloth. Worn-out clothing can be made into dusters, and old wool can be recycled to make fine-grade paper, but most of the synthetic fibres that are common today cannot be used for the latter purpose. If you cannot find a rag dealer, a local office cleaning firm might be interested.

Bulky items

In this category fall many of the items too large to put in the dustbin. They consist of many of the consumer 'durables' especially televisions, refrigerators, washing machines and spin dryers, radios, bicycles, prams, and furniture of all kinds. These account for about 4 per cent of the weight and 8 per cent of the volume of domestic rubbish, but this excludes the largest item you are likely to want to get rid of – the car.

The trouble with bulky refuse is that people too often don't know where to put it and so dump it in woods, ponds and ditches, creating one of the most widespread and abusive impacts on the countryside. Despite fines of up to £100 for the first offence, dumping of bulky refuse continues.

This is to some extent due to the lack of publicity concerning sites available for people to dump their own refuse. Some local authorities provide a free collection and disposal service even though they are not required to do so by law. Others, such as Hammersmith, provide the same service for old cars. However, any car has scrap value and if the car is not very old there is probably an active market for its parts. Try to find a car-breaker who will make proper use of old cars. If you see abandoned vehicles in the streets report them to the Street Inspector's Department of your local Borough Engineer's Office.

ORGANIZE A RECYCLING CLUB

Although most of the reclamation that takes place today relies on industrial and commercial sources that can provide large quantities of homogeneous materials, domestic reclamation has played a significant role in the past.

During World War II it was standard practice to store waste separately, and almost 60 per cent of paper was recycled, But these ideas have been forgotten and the once-flourishing rag-and-bone man has diminished with the advent of synthetic textiles and other non-reclaimable materials.

The growth in environmental awareness, however, can contribute to a renewed interest in the recycling business. In major areas of newsprint, iron, and glass, new opportunities appear to be opening for recycling of home-generated wastes.

Your co-operation is vital to making such efforts work. Municipal refuse is far from homogeneous and it simply is not feasible to separate all of the different materials into different piles once they have been mixed together. Decide which materials you want to recycle and then segregate them at home from the rest of your rubbish. Most of the potentially smelly stuff could go to the compost pile. The newspapers can be accumulated in a stack, magazines in another, cardboard in yet another. Non-returnable glass should first be cleaned, then smashed to reduce the volume, then stored. If you use lots of cans, they should be rinsed out, flattened and stored. If you separate the recyclable materials in this way, storage will be less of a problem because the rubbish is clean and volume is reduced.

Before you accumulate a lot of material, you should line up a market for your collection. Investigate some of the leads listed below. Find out whether any of the service groups or charities such as Shelter have active recycling programes in your area. Unless you combine your materials with your neighbours, it will take a fairly long time to accumulate a large quantity. If you can't find an active programme, start one yourself. It is also a good way to raise money for a worthy cause wherever volunteer labour is available.

SELLING YOUR WASTE

To find a market for your paper, cans, glass, or other junk, try the following:

▪ Look in the yellow pages of your telephone directory under:

  Clothiers – secondhand
  Waste paper merchants
  Scrap metal merchants
  Secondhand dealers
  Salvage merchants
  Waste merchants

▪ Contact your local offices of:

  Aluminium companies
  Breweries
  Glass container manufacturers
  Soft-drink bottling companies
  Steel companies
  Supermarket chains
  Paper manufacturers

▪ Inquire of your local service organizations – the Scouts, amenity, political groups, etc.

▪ Call the Salvation Army.

▪ Find out if your firm – or any you come into contact with – is a member of the National Industrial Materials Recovery Association. Its services, including the excellent monthly journal, 'Industrial Recovery', cost only £5 per year. It is difficult to imagine a better value for money – yet according to Mr Holden, NIMRA Secretary, some large firms terminated their membership when the fee was recently raised to this figure, a sorry commentary on the economic thinking of too many firms. Quite apart from the trivial nature of a £5 debit on the balance sheet of a healthy business, it seems highly probable that firms capitalizing on NIMRA experience and services will recoup their subscription many times over. For more information contact Mr A. W. V. Holden, NIMRA, PO Box 8, 9 Sea Road, Bexhill-on-Sea, Sussex, tel: Bexhill 5018.

For paper try Europe's largest users of waste paper, Thames Board Mill Ltd, Purfleet, Essex, tel: Purfleet 5555.

PROMOTE RE-USE IN YOUR HOUSEHOLD

There are a large number of things you can re-use in your own household. Put some of your 'waste' things to use.

■ There is no reason to buy plastic refuse bags or paper towels for dusting at the same time that you discard perfectly usable paper bags and old clothing that could be used as dusters.

■ Re-use envelopes. Make use of both sides of paper.

■ Return coat hangers to the cleaner instead of throwing them away.

■ Fashion your own Christmas decorations out of bits of metal and paper that you find around the house.

■ Make use of kitchen scraps and leftovers. Boil beef and chicken bones to make soup stock. Skim off the fat and add leftover vegetables and rice, and you will have an appetizing alternative to canned soups.

■ Make your own gravies from meat stock rather than using packaged mixes.

■ Don't throw away beet or radish greens; they can be prepared like spinach. Similarly, other vegetable greens, stalks, and seeds can be cooked and eaten.

■ Recycle your kitchen waste, lawn clippings, leaves and other decomposable organic matter by putting them in a compost pile. Compost is an excellent fertilizer.

■ When your child outgrows his clothes or his toys, pass them on to a friend or relative who can use them, or give them to a charity.

■ Consider buying used goods. Not everything has to be new.

REDUCE CONSUMPTION

Take an inventory of what comes into your home and what leaves it. How many things pass through it essentially unchanged and unused? How many magazines are unread? How many clothes and toys and appliances are thrown out that someone else could use or could be mended if broken?

Despite your best efforts, you will not be able to eliminate entirely your contribution to the municipal waste load. Thus, your second objective should be to make disposal of your share as easy as possible. You can do this in several ways.

■ First, try to stay clear of those materials which are difficult to dispose of. Consult Table 9 in Chapter 8 for a general ranking of the desirability and undesirability of various types of packaging. Plastics, especially PVC, aluminium foils, and composite materials that combine two or more materials in the same package, need a wary eye. Unfortunately, all three of these materials are being used more and more.

■ Aluminium foils are undesirable because they don't degrade, because the aluminium that goes into them is expensive, and because the foil is unreclaimable, for it cannot be separated from the rest of the garbage by any method of mechanical segregation that has been devised to date. The same problem of separation exists with any composite materials.

WASTE THAT ISN'T REFUSE

Not all wastes are solid wastes and not all solid wastes go in the dustbin. We flush a lot of waste down toilets and sinks into the water system and forget about it in the same way we do the rubbish that the dustmen hauls away. We shouldn't. In addition, we send a lot of rubbish into the air when we burn leaves in the autumn or when we burn home refuse. Again we shouldn't. Observe the following rules.

■ Don't flush any waste into the water system that should stay on the land. You shouldn't use a kitchen food waste disposal unit. Compost your organic waste instead.

■ Use non-phosphate, biodegradable detergents and cleaning agents.

■ Don't burn leaves; they should be composted and returned to the soil as fertilizers.

■ Refrain from open burning. It is illegal in many areas because of its contribution to air pollution.

COMPOSTING

The Henry Doubleday Research Association gives the following advice on the different ways of making compost out of your leaves and organic kitchen waste.

The Compost Box

Garden and domestic refuse needs air, water, and shelter to decay into better manure than you can buy. The shelter is all-important both to tidiness and to hold in the heat that makes the difference between compost and a rubbish heap. Choose the site in a sheltered place, which can be in dry shade under trees where nothing much will grow – but in this position your heap will need watering in dry weather. Level off the ground, and flatten it with a spade. Compost heaps are best without concrete or other solid bases. Then make your box, which is topless and bottomless, with a removable front. A ready-made one costs about £5 delivered.

The Bocking Box

This was developed by the Henry Doubleday Research Association as the cheapest do-it-yourself box for non-carpenters. To make it you will need 32 feet of 2-inch mesh wire netting, 3 feet wide, and six wooden stakes about 4 feet in length. The netting should be stapled to all posts on both sides and a brick should be held against the posts to take the shock of the hammering.

Mark the corners of an imaginary 4-foot square at the

centre of the site you have chosen. Then take a 24-foot length of netting and stretch it round three sides of the square, first taking it round the outside of the stakes and then doubling it back round the inside, stapling or tacking it to the stakes as you go. You have now created a three-sided space between two thicknesses of netting with opened-out cartons or newspapers. (This paper will serve as heat insulation. When the paper has decayed sufficiently, it can be composted and replaced with fresh paper.)

For the fourth side of the square – the removable front – take the two remaining stakes and drive each one into the ground directly in front of, and close to, the two stakes which form the open side of the box. When you drive in the two remaining stakes, leave them standing 3 feet 3 inches high. Now take an 8 foot length of netting, double it, and staple it to both sides of the two stakes you have just driven in, so that you create a fourth hollow wall. Take care when you attach the netting that the bottom of it is 3 inches above the ground, thus making the front wall 3 inches higher than the other three walls. Lace the bottom of the netting together so that this wall can be stuffed with paper like the rest. The front needs to be higher off the ground to let air in, and to create a slope when the box is covered with a sheet of corrugated iron to run off excessive rain during the wet season. (Compost heaps can fail from being too wet, which is why composting in pits is not recommended.)

The Wooden Compost Box

A semi-detached box with a compost heap in progress in one half and a heap maturing in the other half is best. Such a box, with two compartments each 3 feet square and 3 feet high, takes 200 feet of 3 inch × ½ inch sawn planks, and six 4 foot lengths of 2 inch × 2 inch timber.

Saw twelve 6 foot planks for the back, and thirty-six 3 foot lengths for the two sides and middle partition. Paint all the wood with Cuprinol, Solignum or other preservative. When dry, begin with the back of the box. Lay three 4 foot lengths in a row, 3 feet apart. Take twelve 6 foot planks, lay them across the three 3 foot lengths, and nail them close together, starting flush at one end of the lengths. This back should now look like a fence 3 feet high by 6 feet long, with three supports extending one foot at the bottom.

Dig three holes 3 feet apart, lift up the back and ram the supports firmly into the ground. Dig three more holes, 3 feet apart, in a row 3 feet in front of the back row. Ram the three remaining 4 foot lengths 9 inches deep into these holes. Nail on the 2 sides and middle partition, using twelve 3 foot lengths for each.

Saw the remaining planks and nail them together using short ends as well, to make 2 removable front sections which will fit immediately behind the upright planks in front of the box.

Building the heap

Start your heap in either type of box by placing two double rows of bricks or brick-ends (an inch apart and 2 feet between the pairs) from front to back so that the ends of these rows stick out under the loose boards of the front or below the wire netting. These provide the draught from below that keeps the 'bacterial bonfire' burning.

Cover the bricks with tough and stemmy rubbish such as privet or lonicera hedge clippings or tall tough weeds to prevent finer materials from blocking the air channels. Then pile on the first 8-inch thick layer of weeds, lawn mowings, and garden wastes, with kitchen refuse in the middle. Then scatter enough dried sludge, dried blood, dried poultry manure, or fishmeal to colour the surface, or a $\frac{1}{2}$-inch layer of rabbit, pigeon, poultry, or other available manure. Add another 8-inch layer of rubbish, whiten this with slaked lime, pile on a third layer then manure or 'activator' again, and so on until the bin is filled. This is rarely possible in a day; most heaps take weeks to build, adding more layers as they sink and decay until the heap is cold and the worms move in. Other signs that compost is ready are a faint earthy odour (the only smell), dark brown or black colour and a crumbly texture like well-rotted farmyard manure. Use it like manure, though it is richer in potash, can be dug in before sowing root crops without making them coarse and forky, and with lime a bucketful a square yard is a fair dressing. Autumn heaps are ready to dig in by spring, spring ones ready before midsummer, and heaps started in June are fine for autumn digging. So with material enough, a bin can be filled and emptied three times a year.

There are many proprietary activators which do not need lime layers, including Q R and Fertosan which need only mixing and watering; Alginure, which is a seaweed jelly in a tin; and Marinure, a dried seaweed powder to be scattered at the rate of 2 oz a square yard of layer. A mixture of 75 per cent of a dried sewage sludge (20 per cent moisture or less, not a wetter one) and 25 per cent Marinure or other seaweed powder fertilizer, is the fastest heating of all. Though layers of soil are often recommended where weeds have soil on the roots, they are unnecessary. (One of the causes of compost producing crops of weed seedlings is not shaking enough soil off.)

What can go in the Compost Heap. Tea-leaves, potato and vegetable peelings of all types, orange and fruit peelings and wastes, egg-shells, fishbones and wastes (not meat bones), rags (except nylon and man-made fibres of any type), paper in small quantities well scattered through the heap, vacuum cleaner dusts, blanket fluff, hair combings, etc.

Brussels sprouts and cabbage stumps will rot if smashed with an axe back. Weed roots such as couch grass, docks, convolvulus and ground elder can be spread on a wire netting rack, laid on concrete, or on the roof of a shed to dry and die. Seeding weeds and diseased materials are safe in the middle of the heap where they get hottest, but smash clubrooted cabbage if used. The heat of a good heap is a safe sterilizer, though if in doubt it is best to occasionally turn the sides of the heap into the middle with a fork to make sure it is all cooked.

What to exclude. Metal milk bottle tops and metal of all

kinds, broken china, and really unrottable wastes, news-papers and cardboard in bulk, man-made fibres, polythene and plastics.

Tree prunings, rose prunings, pine needles, sawdust (except in small quantities), wood shavings, and thick branches from hedges should be excluded though thin chippings will decay, especially if they are used several times. Leather can be composted in time, and if anything fails to rot, or a heap stays partly decayed, use it to start the next one and it usually decays. Grass mowings for composting can often be obtained from council-mown verges, parks and sports grounds, and lawn tennis clubs.

Leafmould making. Dead leaves are the most often wasted of all, when they could make leafmould to add last-ing moisture-retaining humus to any soil.

Leafmould is rather better than peat so far as plant foods are concerned and was chosen at Kew instead of the modern substitute. It carries no vegetable diseases; if it is well made it contains no weed seeds. If there had been any troubles in the soil from its continued use, Kew would have found them after the first century of use.

If you have a shaded, out-of-the-way corner where nothing will grow, this is the place for your leafmould heap, which needs no activator or compost box. Surround your heap with wire netting on stout posts to prevent the leaves blowing round the garden, if the corner is a windy one.

Five cubic yards of leaves stack to three and rot to two, which is roughly a ton of solid humus. Discard dead branches, never include any weeds or green material, and build your stack up to 4 feet high, treading it down firmly and watering it during the first summer if the season is a dry one. Leafmould is not compost; it decays slowly by the action of woodland bacteria and fungi, with a little heat, and by the second spring the heap will be ready to chop down with the spade and use, dug into the flower and vegetable garden, or spread on the surface under shrubs.

Sifted leafmould is excellent in potting soil, and spread over lawns on poor soil it is as good a dressing as it was when Drake played bowls on a leafmould-fed green. Use it in the spring or early autumn at the rate of 1–2 lb a square yard, when the worms have time to take it down to add humus among the grass roots.

Kitchen wastes in winter. If in winter there are too few weeds to cover the kitchen wastes, bury these in the heap. An alternative is to dig pea trenches spade wide and a foot deep, and to cover with soil after each emptying. When a trench is full scatter lime generously on the surface and leave this to wash down until the heap sinks, leaving room to cover spring-sown peas. Potato peelings should not go in pea trenches – odd eyes will grow and crowd the peas unless the winter is very cold.

9. WORKING WITH NATURE

9 WORKING WITH NATURE

If man is to continue living on this planet then the first thing he must develop is a way of living harmoniously with other forms of life.

DRESSED TO KILL

Man is the only animal that kills for vanity. Fashion has been responsible for the extinction of a large number of wild species and for the drastic depletion in numbers of many more.

In the past, the strainer teeth of the baleen whale supplied the whalebone used in corsets and bustles. Millions of birds have been slaughtered just for their feathers, and many species, such as the Chinese egret, are doomed to extinction. Today, the primary concern is over the big cats and other animals that are being killed for their furs and skins.

There were 40,000 tigers in India in 1930; now there are only about 2,000–2,500 more left living in the wild. It needs just 200 more women to crave for, and buy a tiger skin maxi-coat, and the wild tiger will disappear forever.

If it is fashion that has endangered the survival of these species then the creators of fashion – fashion writers, magazines, models, and fur traders – also have the power to restrict consumption before these creatures die out completely.

It probably helps when well-known figures like Danny Kaye or models like Jean Shrimpton pledge themselves not to buy furs or skins of endangered species, but boycotts will never be enough since there are always the few whose vanity matches their greed and irresponsibility.

The International Fur Trade Federation has finally imposed a voluntary ban on the furs of some cat species since they have realized they are cutting off their future supplies by hunting them to extinction. And fur farms and controlled cropping have been developed for various species. The best known is the mink, but the Seals Conservation Act, passed here in June 1970, also provides for rational cropping of seals for their skins, instead of the uncontrolled slaughter that prevailed before.

It is impossible to control some endangered species in their country of origin due to extensive poaching and the difficulty of policing large areas, especially when the monetary incentives for illegal trading are so high. But it is in the consuming country that legal restrictions *must* be enforced. Most countries which *import* the skins of endangered animals have also been slow to make the effort. Look at the case with the Vicuna, where Peru and Bolivia have imposed severe penalties on capture of this animal – whose wool fetches £10 per pound – while Britain has only very recently banned the import of vicuna wool into this country. Other endangered animal skins (usually poached) are still legally allowed into Britain, even when their capture is banned in the country of origin. And Britain still preaches conservation to *other* countries! Britain controls around 85 per cent of the world's fur trade, so pressure for legislation on imported skins here could have worldwide influence.

You do not have to make a contribution to the extinction of any species now endangered.

■ Never buy the skin of the snow or clouded leopard, tiger, cheetah, giant otter or La Plata otter. The International Fur Trade Federation has imposed a ban on trading in these skins.

■ On principle do not buy the skin of anything you know was once wild. This includes most alligator and snake skins. There are quite acceptable alternatives available.

WILDLIFE MANAGEMENT

Wild species of animals are not only cropped for their skins. Loss of habitat through extension of agriculture, forestry, and disturbance are important factors. Pollution, direct poisoning, and trophy hunting also take their toll. The number of zoos in the world has doubled since 1946 and several species, such as the Orang Utan, are in danger of extinction in the wild for the sake of caging the few pathetic survivors. Several species of whale have been hunted to near extinction for their oil to make soap, ambergris for perfume, and the meat for pet foods. Pet food has also taken a severe toll of the Australian kangeroos. Indian rhinoceroses are down to a few hundred because ground rhino horn is thought to restore men's virility. And the list goes on.

Until we learn to care for the continued existence of these species our world is going to be a less diverse and a less stable place to live in. There are some encouraging signs, though. We are beginning to learn the lesson that we are 'cooking our own goose' by allowing species to reach endangered status. The Couprey, a wild relative of the domestic water buffalo could provide the basis for new breeds of domestic stock. The extension of the Vietnam war to Cambodia may have destroyed this possibility but organizations such as FAO are busy working in other parts of the world to develop farming methods using wild game. In many cases wild animals convert grasslands into meat much more efficiently than domestic cattle and are less prone to disease.

International agreements and quota systems have to be devised for common animal resources in danger of extinction, such as the Blue Whale and the Atlantic Salmon. With careful management and understanding there is no reason why many of our wild species should not continue to survive and at the same time supply part of our growing need for food.

WEEDS AND PESTS IN THE GARDEN

Gardening is the closest that most people get to dealing directly with natural systems and it is important that gardeners have some understanding of how nature works.

The essential fact to bear in mind is that natural ecosystems are balanced and generally self-controlling. Each plant, insect, and animal has its place and coexists with the rest of the system. The ecological balance is maintained by a variety of mechanisms, some of them as simple as one species feeding on another, and other mechanisms as subtle as insect sexual attractants and natural, plant-derived insecticides. Most living things are controlled either by predators, by limitations on the supply of an essential factor in their diet, or by competition with other members of the system for living space. In nature there are few animals or pests that eat anything. Each creature usually has a limited range of food sources.

The gardener, like the modern farmer has simplified the natural ecosystem. He grows only a few plant species; such a simple system is an open invitation to any pests that like common garden plants. In a more complex system the vulnerable plants would be protected by the presence of other species of plants for the pest to attack. The pest would also have a harder time finding its target, would have to travel further to infect neighbouring plants, and would have more predators around to pick it off. Thus by reducing diversity the gardener has created instability and increased the chances of his plants being attacked by pests and diseases.

The individual who wants to keep a garden, or even just a

few trees, shrubs, and a lawn, has been led to believe that such a simple endeavour must be accompanied by an all-out war. The enemy is the pest-weed or insect – and the arsenal contains a battery of insecticides, fungicides, miticides, nematicides, and herbicides. The phobia against pests has been carefully cultivated by those who manufacture these chemical products.

Instead of dealing with pest problems intelligently, one is conditioned to reach for the spray at the first sign of an 'invasion' or even, in the absence of any problem, as a 'preventative' measure. The agents that are used are not designed to deal with specific pests. Instead they are broad toxic biocides that wipe out whole systems of plants and insects, the bad ones and the beneficial ones (eg bees and ladybirds) as well. A housekeeper wishing to avoid damaging himself and his environment should keep the following in mind:

▪ Eradication of a pest is generally not a necessary or even desirable goal. Most 'pests' are important to some or other member of the ecosystem, in many cases to one considered 'desirable'.

▪ Eradication of the pest is usually not completely possible anyway, partly because of contamination from other areas, and partly because many of the target pests develop a genetic resistance to the pesticide.

▪ Use of pesticides tends to become addictive. Non-selective chemicals destroy the natural controls, making it easier for the pests to stage a comeback. This leads to more frequent and heavier doses. This speeds the development of resistance so that new (and generally poorly tested) pesticide must be introduced to maintain control. An area so treated can become entirely sterile. And such 'treatment' quickly becomes more expensive than relying on natural controls or putting up with minor pest damage.

▪ To get away from frequent applications the chemical-spray addict tends to rely on long-lived chemicals which retain their toxicity for years. Such persistent pesticides are transported by air or water and thus are now found on virtually every part of the Earth's surface. They concentrate in the bodies of living things, and inevitably reach you through the air you breathe, the water you drink, and the food you eat.

■ Few pesticides have been developed so far that are very selective, ie toxic only to a specific pest and not to other creatures in the ecosystem. To develop selective pesticides is uneconomical for the manufacturers.

■ As our knowledge about them grows, more and more pesticides appear to pose serious threats to human health.

HERBICIDES

With so many organic alternatives chemical weedkillers are best avoided entirely by the home gardener. This is the advice of a growing number of experts. Their advice, however, contrasts sharply with that found in the manufacturers' ads, which tell us that herbicides are a safe and convenient way to deal with weeds.

Weedkillers have been shown to have damaging effects on living things, including man, so it doesn't make sense to assume a given product is safe. Consumer and expert alike must have the answers to a rather large number of questions before a well-informed decision about herbicide use can be made.

Some of the questions are:

- What active ingredients does the product contain?
- What else does it contain that might affect the action of the active ingredient (synergistic effects)?
- Are there any contaminants that could be dangerous?
- Does the product break down into anything that is harmful?
- How long does the herbicide persist in the environment?
- How readily is it transported away from the target area?
- Does it concentrate in particular organisms or localities?
- Does it do the job that it is supposed to do?
- How does it affect non-target organisms?
- What are the short-term effects? Is it acutely toxic?

- What are the long-term effects?
    Does it cause cancer (carcinogenicity)?
    Does it cause birth defects (teratogenicity)?
    Does it cause mutations (mutagenicity)?
- Can the product be applied safely?
- Is the product packaged safely?
- Are the label warnings adequate?
- Do we know enough about it to regard it as safe?

Where are the answers to these questions? Information has been gathered on many of them, but it is woefully incomplete and inconclusive in most respects. The nature of the problem is such that a definite conclusion that a product *is* safe is not possible; there is always the possibility that some effect has been missed. The evidence is always negative – that a product is *not* safe.

Another problem is that most of the experiments have been done with mice and other lab animals, and there is a good deal of uncertainty in the extrapolation of the results to man. Scientists are reluctant to experiment on men, but manufacturers, on the other hand, are experimenting daily with us all. Their 'experiments' are not controlled and it is difficult to sort out the effects. The last question, then, is the critical one. Do we know enough about these products to regard them as safe?

Unfortunately, the two parties who should be in a position to provide a reasonable answer are the manufacturers and the Government. In part, the problem seems to be that the Government has tended to apply the judicial doctrine, innocent until proven guilty, to DDT, 2,4,5-T and who knows what else. The problem is compounded by the slowness with which a product is taken off the market, once the government decides to move.

In April 1970 the Forestry Commission suspended use of 2,4,5-T after 15 years widespread use in this country. The suspension was due to alarming evidence from the USA that this chemical herbicide caused damage to unborn children. No evidence of this sort was submitted by the manufacturers before they put it on the market. The move by the Forestry Commission and the Ministry of Agriculture was surprisingly slow since evidence of its teratogenic (foetus deforming) effects had been building up over the years, especially in the USA, and were published in Britain in 1968. After 22 years of use all that was known about the effects of 2,4,5-T in Britain was its chemical effects on plants, its effects on soil micro-organisms and its toxicity.

The message here is that herbicides are hazardous and that there are practical alternatives for most home uses. Assuming that this is the most ecologically sound viewpoint to adopt, take a look at your own use of herbicides. Weigh the environmental costs and try to see how you can minimize them.

How do you apply herbicides? You may be using them and not know it. Many lawn fertilizers contain herbicides to control lawn weeds. If the fertilizer does its job, the herbicide should not be necessary.

SAFE CONTROL OF WEEDS

A plant is not a weed until someone decides to call it one. According to one definition, a weed is simply a plant in the wrong place. Ecologists tell us that weeds tend to be problems only in ecosystems that have been disturbed; that is, they tend to get crowded out in an ecologically stable system and only appear where new ground is created, vegetation is cleared, or soil is disturbed.

The home gardener can first minimize weed problems by creating a healthy environment for the plants he wants. This is especially true for ground covers (like lawns). In the case of row crops or flower gardens, however, it is desirable to keep the areas between plants free of any vegetation, and this creates an ecologically unstable situation that can be maintained only by artificial means.

The traditional method has always been cultivation – the hoe and the tractor-drawn cultivator. Modern farmers, however, have turned to herbicides (weedkillers) because the expense is lower – but not the environmental costs. The primary domestic application of herbicides has been to control lawn weeds, but they are also used for general gardening purposes.

Before even considering the use of chemical herbicides for the home garden, however, you should try safer methods of weed control. Most home gardens are small enough to make manual weeding a reasonable proposition. Your attitude is important: if digging in the garden is recreation, then weeding will not be much of a chore. If you can keep the soil well tilled and weed regularly, the 'problem' will be minor.

There are many other approaches to weed control without

herbicides and a few of them are given here, provided by the
Henry Doubleday Research Association which specializes
in organic gardening methods.

Lawn weedkillers

The gardener can cut out 2-4-D and other herbicides without hardship, by using an old-fashioned lawnsand. Mix ten
parts of dry sand with seven parts sulphate of ammonia and
three parts sulphate of iron and scatter on the weedy lawn at
a proportion of 4 oz a square yard. A good pinch of this
mixture on the crowns of plantains, dandelions and daisies
will kill them out individually. Up to 8 oz a square yard can
be given to thick patches of clover and pearlwort.

In place of sand, dried sewage sludge of 20 per cent
moisture or less can be used, with the advantage that its
nitrogen acts as a slow feed after the sulphate of ammonia is
spent. A weaker mixture for less weedy lawns is 20 parts
sludge, 3 sulphate of ammonia, and 1 sulphate of iron,
spread at the rate of 8 oz a square yard. Sludge alone at 1 lb
a square yard is a better and far cheaper lawn feed (about
50p per cwt) than any of the chemical lawn tonics containing selective weedkillers.

Home-made lawnsands without selective killers have the
great advantage that it is safe to use the mowings on the
compost heap and as a weed-suppressing surface coat under
bush fruit, roses and shrubs. Underfeeding is one of the
many causes of moss on lawns, and the primary reason is
poor drainage. A most effective moss killer is one pint of
Mortegg winter tar oil wash in eight gallons of water, applied with a rosed can on 32 square yards. The lid of the tin
measures fractions of a pint. A dressing of sludge will encourage the grass to fill in the bare patches this leaves.

The powerful safe weedkiller

Ammonium sulphamate is sold by Boots' branches as
'Amcide' and also direct by Messrs Albright & Wilson,
Knightsbridge Green, London, S.W.1. Roughly speaking it
is sulphate of ammonia whose structure has been altered so

that although it is taken up by the weeds it 'chokes' them and the greedier they are for nitrogen the better it kills. In a fortnight it becomes ordinary sulphate of ammonia and in a month the ground is safe to sow.

Dissolve one lb of the white crystals in a gallon of cold water, in a plastic watering can (it reacts with metals and rusts iron fast) and rose it over 100 square ft (an area ten ft long and ten wide). After about a week the result is complete slaughter. A second watering may be required for large blackberry bushes, but a single go can kill comfrey (in the wrong place), horse radish, couch grass, spear thistles and giant docks.

Only use ammonium sulphamate when weeds are growing strongly in late spring and summer, never autumn or winter, because then the weeds do not gulp it down and choke. Its drawback is cost. A single one lb tin costs 25p but it is cheaper in bulk, and far better to spend money on something powerful and safe for wildlife and yourself, than to spend less and still have weeds.

Do not get it on your skin, in your eyes or let it drain among fish in a pond. Unlike sodium chlorate however, it changes so fast to safe ammonium sulphate that it is rarely washed far through the soil. It has been used by the Forestry Commission to kill rhododendrons under large trees, but it is not a safe killer under surface-rooting subjects like bush fruit. It is of special value for weeds like oxalis or celandine that have quantities of tiny corms, but always wait till they are growing before application.

Sodium chlorate

This is safe for the user and wildlife, but not for plants. There is always a risk that it will soak along through the soil and kill some cherished shrub or tree even when it is used on paths. Used at 1 lb a gallon it is a powerful killer, and about half the price of ammonium sulphamate, but it is not safe to sow or plant for at least six months after use.

It is useful for killing large unwanted comfrey plants, horse-radish and big docks. Slice the root through with a spade just below the surface and spread a heaped tea-spoonful of sodium chlorate on the cut root. This will soak down inside it and kill it to the very tip, without spreading far through the soil. The penetration effect is also used in killing tree stumps. Bore half-inch holes with a brace and bit about an inch in from the bark at six inch intervals round the outside of the stump and 2–3 inches deep. Fill these with sodium chlorate and stopper them with corks. After a fort-night pull out the corks and replace the sodium chlorate. This kills the stump, which will eventually rot away, and prevents honey fungus developing, which can spread to living plants.

NB – Anything soaked in sodium chlorate is inflammable, and there were many cases in the past of gar-deners using it on paths, getting their boots soaked, putting these to dry by the fire, and having them catch light.

Path weedkillers

Where gravel paths cannot be replaced by concrete the safest weedkiller is one pint of tar oil winter wash in 1¼ gal-lons of water, applied with the rose-can thickly enough to wet the weeds thoroughly. A cheaper mixture is a pint of creosote in a gallon of hot water applied in the same way. This will also clear moss off paths.

Killing by cutting, conditions and cultivations

Perennial nettle and bracken can be killed by repeated cut-tings. Use a rough grass cutter such as a Hayter, or a scythe on them in May, July, and September, roughly every six weeks and rake up the material for compost. In three years you will have killed them and will miss their supply. Lime the ground well to alter the conditions so their seedlings will not return.

Marestail (*Hippuris vulgaris*) thrives on ill-drained sub-soils and poor clays, so though ammonium sulphamate will kill it, the seedlings will appear again. First drain the garden if you can, digging out a pond if your clay is too solid for a soak-away. If the soil is not so much damp as poor and acid clay, spread as much as 4lb a square yard of slaked lime and distribute it through the top eight inches with a rotary cultivator in summer. With this a two-inch layer of spent mushroom compost or 5 lb a square yard of a dried sludge can go in to add humus and plant foods. Both can go on with lime. If farmyard manure or deep-litter compost are used there will be a chemical reaction, and all the nitrogen wastes in the smell of ammonia. Put the lime on first, and these at least a month later.

Couchgrass can be killed by rotary cultivation three times during summer. To chop up the roots and dry them out once, is useless, a second go a month later is good, and a third makes a real job. The man with a new house on a grass field would do well to put off gardening until he has killed his weeds, and got his digging done by a local man with a powerful machine, like a Howard Gem or 600, not a plough which has not the same weedkilling action.

Mulching

This is a method of spreading a coat of something organic on the surface to prevent weed germination, but many perennial weeds will grow through the thickest coat of almost anything. The cheapest mulch is lawn mowings, and if the lawn is mown with normal frequency there should be no trouble with seedling grasses. Never spread any mulch before the soil has had time to warm, about mid-April, and keep the mowings away from stems.

With these precautions mowings are ideal between bush fruit, either along or with manure or cut comfrey under them, under roses and shrubs, and between pea and tomato rows. They should not be used round anything slug attacked, because surface mulches encourage slugs as all 'no-diggers' know.

Baled peat is often used but is very expensive in the quantities needed, but home made leaf-mould, is free. You must think ahead, however, because it must be well rotted – which takes at least a year. Straw composted with horse manure and gypsum plus some sterilized soil is excellent and can often be bought cheaply. Though it may contain pesticide residues, pyrethrum is usually used against fungus gnats. For alpines, and as a manure rather than a mulch, use Pompost, which is composted apple waste from making cider vinegar, weedfree and splendid humus, but at 75p for 50 lb, better value than municipal compost, because it is all humus, without ashes or broken glass.

Straw in bales which come apart in 'slices' about six inches thick, is a good weed suppressor. If it can be left on till it decays it will even kill creeping buttercup, but it is expensive today, and untidy in the average garden. A load of manure costs less and is better value.

Annual weedkillers

There are two important weed types – annual and perennial, and the major difference between plants and weeds is that the latter seed fast (a chickweed seedling an inch high can produce seed) and their seeds are designed to germinate at intervals over a period of years. Lush annual weeds preserve soil nitrogen and are good green manure dug in before they seed, and all are good compost material.

A flame gun is like a blowlamp, but though the advertisements say it 'Kills all weeds instantly', it does not. It scorches up the annual ones, wasting their humus, and the release of nitrogen from the surface soil sterilization acts as a tonic for the perennial weeds that it does *not* kill.

If weeds on an uncultivated area are far ahead towards seeding and there is no time even to cut them for compost, buy a Farm Disinfectant (Boots do a good one), containing 40-50 per cent Phenols. Mix a pint in a two gallon can of cold water and water it on with a fine rose to wet the foliage only. If a round rose, as used for watering seedlings, is employed it can be kept off the rows and used to kill the cresslike germination of seedlings that comes from compost that failed to heat enough to kill its weed seeds.

PESTICIDES

The situation with the pesticides – insecticides, miticides, nematocides, fungicides, and rodenticides – is similar to that with herbicides, except that many of the pesticides are more persistent and less selective.

The chlorinated hydrocarbons – DDT, Aldrin, Chlordane, BHC (benzene hexachloride and lindane), TDE, Dieldrin, Endrin, Heptachlor, Methoxychlor, and Toxaphene – are notorious for their persistence. The use of aldrin, dieldrin and DDT restricted now by voluntary agreement here are banned in the USA, Denmark and some other countries. Their replacements have been organic phosphates and carbamates. These tend to be less persistent, which is an advantage; however, non-persistence in itself does not mean they are harmless, as some advertising or poor labelling might indicate. The organic phosphates, in fact, include the most toxic of the pesticides, such as Parathion which are also non-selective. In fact, use of malathion and parathion caused 600 deaths in Japan from 1958–63.

The best precaution is not to use any of these chemical pesticides, for they are no real substitute for non-polluting pest controls.

PESTICIDES TO AVOID

Here are a few of the pesticides that one should avoid at all costs; this list is by no means exhaustive.

▪ Arsenic in any form – used in insecticides, rodenticides, and herbicides. A cumulative poison in animals and soil. Can render soil permanently sterile. Carcinogenic.

▪ Mercury (organic and inorganic) – widely used as a fungicide to preserve seeds, and on golf courses. Wildlife eat treated seed and become unsafe for human consumption. Several instances of human poisoning via this route. Mercury of industrial origin has contaminated many of our inland waterways and consequently the fish.

▪ The persistent hydrocarbons (DDT, Aldrin, BHC, lindane, DDD, Dieldrin, Endrin, Heptachlor, Toxaphene). DDT is notorious. The others should be notorious too. Chlordane, for instance, is sometimes recommended but should never be used casually and is now restricted.

SAFE PESTICIDES

General Pesticides. Any good garden shop should sell derris and pyrethrum. There are many makes of both and mixtures of the two are stronger than either separately. They are capable of killing caterpillars and a range of pests including aphides of all types listed on the tin or bottle. They are sometimes mixed with lindane and other organo-chlorine compounds and these should be refused. Derris is available as a dust that is most effective against the fleabeetle which eats holes in the leaves of brassica plants and radishes. As it began as a Malay fish poison do not let it trickle in the goldfish pond. If you keep bees and have to spray anything in flower, use pyrethrum in the evening and it will have killed your aphides and be harmless by the time your bees start work in the morning.

Quassia – the Safest Pesticide. Quassia has the advantages of cheapness, of not killing the ladybirds which are eating your aphides, and of sparing bees when sprayed against apple sawfly or raspberry beetle caterpillars, at blossom time. It is chips of the wood of *Picrasma quassioides* which keep dry for years in a tin, and can only be ordered through a good chemist because it is still used by District Nurses to kill nits in children's hair. Boil 4 oz (a pound costs about 20p) in a gallon of water for two hours, pour off the yellow liquid when cool and dilute with five parts of water for an all-round garden spray for aphides and small caterpillars. A 1-to-3 mixture will kill gooseberry sawfly caterpillars that can strip the leaves from a bush in four days.

Home-made Pesticides – Nicotine. The cheapest powerful pesticide is nicotine, which is now difficult to buy, but is easily made by boiling 4 oz of non-filter-tip cigarettes (or $\frac{1}{2}$ lb of filter-tips) in a gallon of water for half an hour. Strain the clear brown liquid through a nylon stocking and it will keep several weeks in a stoppered bottle. Dilute with four parts of water to one of nicotine for an anti-caterpillar spray or for anything hard to kill.

Water it along rows of young peas and beans when their leaves are eaten out of shape by the pea and bean weevil, a tiny beetle that is clay-coloured and hides under clods so you rarely see it. Mix a quart of the solution with 1 oz of soft soap or soapflakes and spray on spring cabbage plants, broccoli and late brussel sprouts in the autumn to kill mealy cabbage aphid, cabbage whitefly and cabbage moth caterpillars before they burrow in the hearts. This strength kills celery and chrysanthemum leaf miners.

If you have a *Euonymus* hedge, syringe it thoroughly with nicotine in November to kill the hibernating caterpillars of the small ermine moth which are the curse of these hedges, and the winter stage of the blackfly on broad beans. These also winter on viburnus (all species), and if everyone sprayed these we might wipe out this pest. Squirt nicotine hard into the gnarled bark at the base of old rose bushes in November because it is here that greenfly hibernate.

Non-smokers can obtain ashtray emptyings from cinemas and public houses, and the best way to keep free nicotine is in the form of cigarette ends in a tin. Do not spray it on anything you are going to eat within a fortnight, so the rain can wash it off, and label any that is ready boiled 'POISON'. It breaks down quickly in the soil, unlike DDT and other organo-chlorine compounds. Though nicotine costs nothing when made from boiled cigarette ends it is a powerful poison, so wash your hands after using it.

Home-made Pesticides for Aphides. For greenfly on roses use something weaker. Cut up 3 lb of rhubarb leaves, boil for half an hour in three quarts of water and strain. When cool dissolve 1 oz of soapflakes in a quart of water, mix the two and use as a general spray for any aphis. It can also be made with 3 lb of elder leaves; this mixture was used in the past as a spray for mildew on roses.

Bordeaux Mixture. This is still the best and safest preventative for Potato Blight in potatoes and tomatoes, to be sprayed on every fortnight from mid-June till the end of September, especially in cold, wet summers. Most gardeners gamble on missing it, and there are resistant potato varieties, but no resistant tomatoes, other than the tiny 'red currant' varieties. It can still be bought ready to mix and should be used according to the directions on the tin.

Burgundy Mixture. Make this fresh always by dissolving 3 oz of copper sulphate in a gallon of water in a plastic bucket (copper sulphate reacts with zinc), so leave overnight to cool and finish dissolving. Stir 4 oz of washing-soda into a gallon of cold water, mix the two and spray, but never on anything with leaves. Protect near evergreens with polythene.

This is an excellent scab killer for apples and pears with the great advantage over lime sulphur that many varieties are 'sulphur shy' and if you do not know what your trees are, you are safe with Burgundy Mixture. Spray it on gooseberries in January against mildew spores, peaches in February or March, just as the blossom buds begin to swell, against leaf curl and leaf blister, and on roses in December and January against mildew spores. It has another great advantage over lime-sulphur in sparing *Anthocoris nemorum*, one of our best and most versatile pest-eaters, so by giving up winter tar oil washes and using Burgundy, you are saving a friend.

Lime-Sulphur. This can be bought ready-made and used according to the directions on the tin, but read carefully to see that it has no expensive and deadly additions. Though it can be used against rose mildew at one part to 60 its most valuable use is to spray on black currants at the rate of one pint to $2\frac{1}{2}$ gallons when the first leaves are the size of shillings (5p), to catch the big bud mite which is spreading then. Pick off and burn all big buds, which are quite distinctive, not only because the mites weaken the bush, but they carry Reversion – a genuine virus.

ECOLOGICAL PEST CONTROL

Hopefully natural controls will provide the main means of controlling pests in the future. As scientists gain a better understanding of how natural controls operate, we should depend less and less on the chemical pesticides that have proven so destructive and attack living organisms so indiscriminately. A promising technique is the use of *natural predators*. The desirability of frogs and birds is well known. Some beneficial insect predators are commercially available and control by distributing pest predators is already done for the red mite in cucumber houses.

There are other methods being developed that offer advantages over the presently available methods of pest control. Some of them will probably be used only by the professional exterminator, but others will become commercially available. Juvenile insect hormones can be used in very small amounts to prevent insects from maturing into adult pests. Insect sex attractants can be used to lure pests into traps where they can be readily killed. Another approach involves sterilizing male insects in large numbers by irradiation and releasing them to mate with the wild females, a technique already used with considerable success. Recent research indicates that it may be possible to breed the sterile males.

10. CONSUMER POWER

10   CONSUMER POWER

The conversion to a life style more related to the ability of the Earth to supply our needs must start by the consumer regaining the political power of the individual to have real choice in the market place. This must be created by the will-power and determination of those who are prepared to overcome their inbred habits and years of unecological living. Start today.

Begin in the home and at the market; try using some of the ideas in this book. Conserve power and water and paper and metals. Look for products that come in returnable packages. Find a market for your used newspapers. Begin to say no to some of the products that are ecologically unsound – simply don't buy them.

INFORMATION FOR THE CONSUMER

Consumer influence most often depends on good information. The introduction already mentioned some of the difficulties the consumer faces in trying to find out the environmental effects of different products. What then can the consumer, with so many uncertainties and without specialist knowledge, do? He can try to learn more about environmental issues and the impact of the goods he buys, and at the same time maintain a healthy scepticism about the sources of his information.

This means, for instance, recognizing the bias that such firms as Shell or Ford will each bring into the debate over how much it will cost to reduce lead pollution from car exhaust. It means keeping in mind the vested interests of organizations such as the Institute of Petroleum, which are not unbiased research groups but institutes set up by the manufacturers to collectively protect their own interests and profits. Even the professional societies, ideally supposed to be objective and careful in making judgements, frequently represent narrow points of view in their public news releases and trade journals.

Unfortunately, government has too often failed to live up to its role of impartial protector of the public interest. In a sense, this failing is built into our system of representative government. A politician is going to be in favour of a factory if it gives employment in a depressed area that is his own constituency. The same goes for local government, where more industry means more rate revenue. It is a natural position for any politician sensitive to his electors. But beyond this one should recognize that 'our' representatives represent more than just us – business, industry, trade unions and parts of the government bureaucracy compete as constituents, and often have a more direct line to our elected officials than we do. This is especially true of government regulatory groups or committees which have seemed in some cases to become advocates for those they are meant to regulate.

Politicians also like to follow the fortunes of different industries for personal reasons. James Callaghan once said 'I do not think of them as the honourable member for X or Y or Z. I look at them and say "Investment Trusts". "Capital Speculators" or "That is the fellow who is the Stock Exchange man who makes a profit on gilt edge".' MPs have to declare a direct interest, such as directorship of a company, but shares and other interests can easily be transferred to wives and relatives.

These generalizations are not meant to imply that all industry and government sources are unreliable. Many are genuinely concerned about the environmental consequences of the decisions they make. These points are made because you, as a consumer of goods and services, also becomes a user of information in making your product choices. You must size up your sources of information as you would the salesman who tries to sell you a used car. The appendix on sources of information can help you further in contacting sources of up-to-date information.

WATCH OUT FOR ECO-PORNOGRAPHY

Too often the 'solution' to pollution by an industry is to try
to convince the public it doesn't exist. Thus serious environmental problems which should be openly discussed are
given to the public relations department instead of to an
engineer or ecologist. Now that environmental issues are in
the daily news, people are beginning to look at their surroundings and ask questions. It is often the job of public
relations men to supply publicity answering their own irrel-
evant questions or totally obscuring the issue. Sometimes
product advertisements say good things for the wrong
reason, and you will always find someone advertising his
solution to pollution if he thinks he can sell more, or make
money out of it. Friends of the Earth is compiling a list of
eco-pornographic advertisements and statements – please
send along any you find.

LOCAL GROUP ACTION

One of the few ways of getting widespread change for a better environment can be through a powerful consumer movement. The Consumers' Association and local consumer groups are doing a good job, but very rarely do they look into the environmental costs of consumer goods, nor do they suggest that purchasing be restricted in any way.

One way you can make at least a local impact is to wage a campaign among housewives in your area and systematically pick out the products, stores and factories which ignore the environmental costs. Basically, education and consumer boycott should be the groundwork for local group action. Activate existing groups such as Women's Institutes as well. Prepare 'fact sheets' from the information given in these pages and get them circulated to members of groups you belong to, or to your friends.

Be prepared to demonstrate – start by returning the non-returnable bottles and leave excess packaging at the place where you bought it. The last thing companies like to see is effectively organized power.

Remember too, that any organized religion is also a political organization responsible to grass-roots pressure. Give this book to your local vicar, ask him to preach a sermon on it and discuss its contents among the congregation.

CO-OPERATIVE ACTION

If the national Co-operative movement which exists in this country, started an environmental policy which provided people with genuine alternatives to environmentally bad products, it could turn into a mass movement. Money from profits could be spent on supporting local environmental education, and, by boycotts and price incentives, consumption could be redirected to ecologically sounder products.

You do not need much initiative, though, to set up your own buyers' co-operative. Families living in blocks of flats or groups of friends can often buy in bulk or can organize the sharing of consumer goods. The future tendency may be more towards integrated economic groupings of families rather than integrated social units, so help it along. Several families could use one vacuum cleaner, or washing machine – it all helps in the right direction.

YOUTH

Youth is the only sector of the population from which a significant proportion of people can be found who are not prepared to accept that material wealth brings them any nearer to satisfying their basic needs. Thus, many reject the excesses of an over-consuming society.

Pop stars are beginning to introduce environmental issues into their songs. Some of them, such as songs by Donovan, or 'The Big Yellow Cab' by Joni Mitchell, with its line 'They paved paradise and put up a parking lot' have reached the Top Ten. Unfortunately, most modern singers make money out of saying the right things – and they then spend it on making the problems worse. Also, it is not usually the words of their songs that teenagers copy, but the wasteful consumption rate of their idols. Pop groups and others could do more to put their money where their mouths are.

I have always been struck by the complex and expensive equipment available to students at university and the vast potential for using it to do something for the community. Most departmental student societies organize programmes of more of the same boring lectures that they curse every day. What about product testing as a useful laboratory activity? Pollution Probe at Toronto University does this and tested all Canadian detergents for their environmental effects. Monitoring of industrial pollution would also be a very useful exercise if properly co-ordinated.

HOUSEWIVES

Much of this book applies to you. At the same time much of its impact will depend upon you. It is the housewife who not only consumes for herself, but buys a large proportion of the family's items of consumption, washes most of their clothes, and disposes of their rubbish. It is she who collectively can do the most to reduce the effects of the production, use, and disposal of consumer goods on the deteriorating quality of our environment.

APPENDIX I

BIBLIOGRAPHY BY CHAPTER

CHAPTER 1. INTRODUCTION

Consumers

Knox F., *Consumers and the Economy*, Harrap (£1.25p)

Roberts, E., *Consumers*, Watts, 1966 (£1.25p)

Roberts, E., *Consumer Protection: Is anybody listening?* in a Penguin Survey: Business and Industry, 1967 (42½p)

Law for Consumers, Consumer's Association, 1970

Environment

Arthur, D., *Survival*, English University Press, (£1·40p)

Arvill, R., *Man and Environment*, Penguin Books, 1969 (55p)

Barr, J., *The Assault on Our Senses*, Methuen, 1970 (£2·50p)

Barr, J., *The Environmental Handbook*, Ballantine/FOE, 1971 (40p)

Commoner, B., *Science and Survival*, Ballantine Books, 1971 (40p)

Dansereau, P. (ed) *Challenge for Survival*, Columbia University Press, 1970 (£3·60p)

CHAPTER 2. OVER-CONSUMPTION

Galbraith, J. K. , *The Affluent Society*, Penguin Books

Packard, V., *The Wastemakers*, Penguin Books, 1960 (35p)

Packard, V., *The Hidden Persuaders*, Penguin Books, 1957 (30p)

Standinger, Dr J. J. P., *Disposal of Plastic Waste and Litter*, Society of Chemical Industry, 1970

CHAPTER 3. POPULATION AND FOOD CONSUMPTION

Population

Allison, A. (ed), *Population Control*, Penguin Books, 1970 (35p)

Bougstrom, G., *Too Many: A Study of the Earth's Biological Limitations*, Collier-Macmillan, 1969 (£2·10p)

Ehrlich, P. and A., *Population, Resources, Environment*, W. H. Freeman, 1970 (£4·20p)

Ehrlich, P., *The Population Bomb*, Ballantine Books (30p)

Hardin, G., *Population, Evolution and Birth Control*, W. H. Freeman, 1969 (£2·50p) paperback (£1·20p)

Taylor, L. R. (ed), *The Optimum Population for Britain*, Academic Press, 1970 (£1·75p)

Food

Huxley, E, *Brave New Victuals*, Chatto and Windus, 1965 (£1·05p)

Report on Aldrin and Dieldrin Residues in Food, Food Additives and Contaminants Committee, HMSO, 1967

CHAPTER 4. START WITH WHERE YOU LIVE

Town Planning: The Consumers' Environment, Research Institute for Consumer Affairs.

Noise

Bell, Dr A., *Noise*, World Health Organization, Geneva, 1966 (50p)

Burns, W., *Noise and Man*, John Murray, 1968 (£2·50p)

Goodson, W., 'Noise – ban it from your home', *Do it yourself Magazine,* December, 1961

Noise Abatement Society, *The Law on Noise,* 1969 (£1·05p)

Rodda, M., *Noise and Society,* Oliver and Boyd, 1967 (40p)

CHAPTER 5. LIQUID ASSETS

Water

Southgate, B A., *Water: Pollution and Conservation,* Thunderbird Enterprises (£2·00p)

Seventh Annual Report of the Water Resources Board, HMSO, 1970 (70p)

Eleventh Progress Report of The Standing Technical Committee on Synthetic Detergents, HMSO, 1971 (20p)

Household Detergents. A report on the supply of household detergents by the Monopolies Commission, HMSO, 1969 (53p)

CHAPTER 6. ALL POWER POLLUTES

Crowe, S., *The Landscape of Power,* Architectural Press, 1958 (£1·00p)

Simpson, E. S., *Coal and the Power Industries in Postwar Britain,* Longmans (87p)

CHAPTER 7. TRANSPORT: WHERE IS IT TAKING US?

Bowers, P. H. and Sherwood, P. T., *Air Pollution from Road Traffic – a Review of The Present Position,* Road Research Laboratory, Ministry of Transport, 1970

Buchanan, C. D., *Mixed Blessings: The Motor in Britain*, Leonard Hill, 1958 (£2·25p)

Buchanan, C. D., *Traffic in Towns*, Penguin Books, 1964 (55p)

Road Research Laboratory, *A Review of Road Traffic Noise*, Ministry of Transport, 1970

Tetlow, J. and Goss, A., *Home, Towns and Traffic*, Faber, 1968 (£2·50p)

CHAPTER 8. WASTED WEALTH

Ellis, H. M., *Solid Waste Disposal*, Council of Europe, Strasburg, 1967

Refuse Disposal, report for the 'Countryside in 1970 Conference', Royal Society of Arts (20p)

CHAPTER 9. WORKING WITH NATURE

Wildlife

Dorst, J., *Before Nature Dies*, Collins, 1970 (£3·15p), softcover (£1·90p)

Guggisberg, C. A. W., *Man and Wildlife*, Evans Brothers, 1970 (£3.50p)

Gardening and Pesticides

Carson, R., *Silent Spring*, Hamish Hamilton, 1963 (£1·25p); Penguin Books, 1965 (25p)

Graham, F., *Since Silent Spring*, Hamish Hamilton, 1970 (£2·00p). To be published by Pan/Ballantine, January 1972, 40p

Herber, L., *Our Synthetic Environment*, Cape, 1963 (£1·25p)

Hunter, B., *Gardening Without Poisons*, Hamish Hamilton, 1965 (£1·25p)

Mellanby, K., *Pesticides and Pollution*, Collins, 1967 (£1·50p); paperback – Fontana, 1969 (45p)

Rudd, R, *Pesticides and The Living Landscape*, Faber, 1965 (£1.75p)

APPENDIX II

FURTHER SOURCES OF INFORMATION

One of the most difficult problems for the concerned consumer is how to get information on which to base his detailed buying strategy. This guide can only give directions and cannot in any way be considered comprehensive.

Information from the trade

For many of the consumer sections in this book there will be special trade journals or trade associations. Most of these can be found from a reference source such as Whitaker's Almanac. Some public libraries have commercial reference sections where you can look through the trade journals.

Consumer organizations

Consumers' Association

Put out a monthly magazine called WHICH? containing reports on their tests carried out on a wide range of consumer goods. Another similar magazine FOCUS was put out by the Consumer Council but this was discontinued when the council was closed by the Government. While neither of the magazines has an environmental focus – some of their recommendations in fact run counter to the best interest of the environment – they contain a large amount of information that is useful in making ecologically sound consumer decisions. Recently some issues of WHICH? have contained reports on environ-

mental problems such as the report on air pollution in
WHICH?, November 1969.
14 Buckingham Street,
London, W.C.2.
Tel: 01–839 1222

National Innovation Centre
Has a magazine called WHAT which occasionally contains
relevant information; and it will follow up your practical
ideas for recycling, etc. It may be setting up a Consumer
centre as well since the Consumer Council has closed.
Bedford Chambers, King Street, Covent Garden,
London WC2E 8HA
Tel: 01–836 8967

Research Institute for Consumer Affairs
Does independent research and testing on consumer products. They also produce a series of reports on their
findings.
43 Villiers Street,
London, W.C.2.
Tel: 01–930 3360

Environmental groups

No environmental groups cover the broad range of topics
which relate to the environmental effects of consumer goods
but several of them pick out certain aspects and these may
be found below. Friends of the Earth have established a
consumers group and produce fact sheets on certain products and consumer topics.

Conservation Society
Aims to reverse 'increasing degradation of the environment' by population stabilization and more responsible
use of technology. Promotes conservation of natural resources, animal life as part of man's natural environment.
21 Hanyard's Lane, Cuffley,
Potters Bar, Herts
Tel: 01–284 2517
Secretary: S. C. Lawrence

Friends of the Earth (FOE) Ltd, UK
A non-profit organization for aggressive political and legislative activity aimed at restoring the environment.
8 King Street,
London, W.C.2.
Tel: 01–836 0718
Chairman: Barclay Inglis

Henry Doubleday Research Association
Promotes gardening without the use of chemical fertilizers or poison sprays. Provides an essential source of continuing information for gardeners.
20 Covent Lane,
Bocking,
Braintree, Essex
Tel: Braintree 1483
Secretary: L. D. Hills

Keep Britain Tidy Group
A voluntary organization aiming to make Britain cleaner, tidier and more beautiful.
86 The Strand,
London, W.C.2.
Tel: 01–836 6463.
Secretaries: Miss Goodman and Miss Moss

Noise Abatement Society
Aims to eliminate excessive and unnecessary noise from all sources by taking all possible steps under the existing laws to protect the public from assault by noise; to inform the public by every means of the dangers of noise to health, and of their legal rights against those who create noise; to press for enforcement of present laws against noise and for new byelaws where existing laws appear inadequate.
6 Old Bond Street,
London W.1.
Tel: 01–493 5877
Secretary: John Connell

Royal Commission on Environmental Pollution

Established by the Government in 1970 'to advise on matters, both national and international, concerning the pollution of the environment: on the adequacy of research in this field; and the future possibilities of danger to the environment'.

Great George Street,
London, S.W.1.
Tel: 01–930 3324
Secretary: Miss D. M. Wilde

Soil Association

Brings together those working for a fuller understanding of the vital relationships between soil, plant, animal and man. Initiates, coordinates, and assists research in this field. Collects and distributes the knowledge gained so as to create a body of informed public opinion.

Walnut Tree Manor,
Haughley, Stowmarket, Suffolk
Tel: 044–970–235/7
Secretary: Sir Ronald Garvey

Town and Country Planning Association

Fights for 'humanity in planning'; advocates national land-use policy to safeguard green belts and farmland. Promotes policies of dispersal and growth in New Towns; and informs public of planning issues.

17 Carlton House Terrace,
London, SW1Y 5AS
Tel: 01–930 8903
Director: David Hall

World Wildlife Fund (British National Appeal)

Dedicated to saving threatened wildlife throughout the world. Working on the conservation of endangered species by raising funds for projects and purchasing reviews. They also produce a bulletin and a magazine, *Wildlife News,* which gives up-to-date information on use of wildlife for food and furs.

7–8 Plumtree Court,
London, E.C.4.
Tel: 01–353 2615
Information Officer: Ted Scrope-Howe

Environmental Periodicals

The Ecologist (monthly), Subscriptions Department, Darby
   House, Bletchingley Road, Merstham, Surrey (£3·00p p.a.)
Your Environment (quarterly), Subscriptions Department,
   10 Roderick Road, London, N.W.3. (£1·75p p.a.)

Population Groups

The Family Planning Association
   Set up as a charitable trust providing information and
   advice on family planning and related matters.
   Your local authority may provide a Family Planning
   Centre or alternatively there may be a Brook Advisory
   Centre, in your city.
   Margaret Pyke House,
   27/35 Mortimer Street,
   London, W1A 4QW
   Tel: 01–636 7866

Birth Control Campaign
   Has been set up independently to act as a pressure group
   for more birth control facilities, to promote education and
   research and for legislative reform.
   233 Tottenham Court Road,
   London, W.1.
   Tel: 01–580 9360

Conservation Society
   Has also actively been involved in population issues. They
   have produced several pamphlets on population including
   'Why Britain needs a Population Policy', which can be
   obtained for 5p, post free, from The Conservation
   Society.

ACKNOWLEDGEMENTS

Most of this book is based on the American version called *The User's Guide to the Protection of the Environment* so the first debt of gratitude goes to Paul Swatek who did the tremendous job of getting it together, and to Friends of the Earth, USA, who produced it.

The Consumers' Association assisted with the generous use of their library and photocopying facilities, and Walter Patterson of 'Your Environment' gave useful comments and suggestions. Lawrence Hills of the Henry Doubleday Research Association provided me with a great deal of gardening information, some of which is reproduced in the text. The research material and manuscript could not have been got together without the assistance of Jean Gardner and others from Friends of the Earth, UK.

FRIENDS OF THE EARTH

The present environmental crisis is only now being recognized as an ultimate threat to man's survival. We are finally becoming aware that the land, sea, and air on which we depend cannot tolerate the sort of abuse to which they have been subjected.

Action is required now to develop a way of life based on sound ecological principles and related to the limited capacity of the Earth to support the human species. To place our faith in growth of the Gross National Product as a measure of our welfare and happiness, and in technological solutions to all our problems, is proving disastrous to the environment.

It is one thing, though, to lament the tragedy of dying rivers and the curse of industrial dereliction, but quite another to choose an issue, fight the case, and win. Any campaign for a better environment must make sure this is an issue which decides the fate of politicians, activates complacent authorities, or closes factories.

This situation needs new organizations uncompromising in their defence of the environment and uninhibited in the action they are prepared to take.

Friends of the Earth Ltd is one of them. It is an international non-profit making organization prepared to take aggressive legal and political action to ensure a better environment for everyone. In the UK it is formed as a company limited by guarantee, so as to fight freely and quickly.

We are not just idealists, but we do have ideals. We place emphasis on practical action and we recognize the need for many new organizations to share the work. We are also aware of the need to give more help to existing conservation groups, which have been labouring long and hard. Our Earth is threatened and needs every friend it has.

FOE intends firstly to pursue an active publishing programme with Ballantine Books, to provide the best possible information, written for the intelligent layman, about the remedial action required to meet current threats to the environment. We intend to encourage further research aimed at a greater understanding of the impact on the Earth of man and his technological society. We shall also urge action now, based on what is already known, to resist the use of a given technology without proof that it will not cause lasting harm.

Unhampered by any party-political allegiance, FOE will undertake substantial legislative activity, including lobbying and focusing public attention on critical issues. We will join other organizations in going to court to fight environmental abuse. We shall wage an all-out war on any interest which ignores the needs of the environment.

FOE's members will form specific task forces supported by teams of environmental experts and citizen's groups. The acronym FOE is appropriate: any friend of the Earth must be the foe of whatever or whoever degrades the Earth.

FOE needs support. It has a growing register of Friends who are prepared to fight authorities and industries insensitive to the ecological effects of their activities. If these goals are yours, contact us by completing the form on the following page and sending it to Friends of the Earth, 8 King Street, London, WC2E 8HS. Tel. 01-836 0718.

FRIENDS OF THE EARTH
REGISTRATION FORM

Registration as a Friend   ......
Friend and Supporter £3   ......
Friend and Supporter £100   ......

Name: ....

Address: ....

....

Tel. No: (day) .... (evening)..........

Interests and/or specialized
knowledge or training:

Ideas for action:

All cheques should be made payable to Friends of the Earth
Ltd. As a company limited by guarantee, all money FOE
receives must be devoted to its objects and cannot be distributed.

Friends of the Earth, 8 King Street, London,
WC2E 8HS.

Take a thoughtful look at the way we live nowadays

your environment
quarterly subscription magazine
discusses the contemporary problems in depth and detail and provides a continuing consumers' guide to environmental issues.

Subscribers represent a broad spectrum of readers with professional and lay interest in environmental issues – in rational technology, good design, socially responsible management and ecological conservation.

If you would like to subscribe and join the list of readers in more than 30 countries round the world please send us the coupon below, or write for further details.

....

To: *your environment*, 10 Roderick Road, London NW3 2NL.
   please enter my subscription for one year at £2·00
   for four issues, including postage.*
   ... To begin current issue   ... Payment enclosed
   ... To include back issues   ... Please send invoice
     as available

Cheques and postal orders to *your environment*, please.
*USA, $6, other overseas £2·00, including post paid seamail letter rate; airmail rates on application.

Name: ....

Address: ....

....

INDEX

MORE BALLANTINE CONSERVATION TITLES

The Environmental Handbook
edited by John Barr   40p

The 1970s is our last chance for a future that makes ecological sense. The book focuses on some of the major problems of our deteriorating environment, and – more important – suggests action that can be taken immediately in any community by any individual. Foreword by Kenneth Allsop, contributors include Sir Frank Fraser Darling, Dr Paul Ehrlich, Lord Ritchie-Calder, Professor René Dubos and Dr Kenneth Mellanby.

The Population Bomb
Dr Paul R. Ehrlich   30p

Overpopulation is now the dominant problem in all our personal, national, and international planning. Dr Ehrlich clearly describes the dimensions of the crisis in all aspects, and provides a realistic evaluation of the remaining options.

Wilderness and Plenty
Sir Frank Fraser Darling   30p

In his 1969 Reith Lectures, Sir Frank Fraser Darling views the wilderness as a shrinking natural resource, no longer an environment to be conquered by man. He looks towards the future with a plan for conservation and a plea for man's responsibility to nature.

How to be a Survivor
Dr Paul R. Ehrlich and Richard L. Harriman   40p

The 1970s is the decade of decision, and in this decade mankind will either take the necessary action to preserve his species on the surface of this planet, or he will so erode, overtax, and exploit his only habitat that he will destroy himself. This is a plan to save Spaceship Earth, and it is up to those with the intellect, guts, and resources to recognize what is needed and to convince and carry the rest of the world. If we can do this, mankind will have a chance.

Science and Survival
Barry Commoner   40p

An eminent ecologist speaks out on survival in the 70s. This book is an urgent warning of the dangers we face from new scientific and technological advances which will have harmful long-range effects on our environment. Only by recognizing these dangers can we safeguard a future for ourselves.

This and the other books advertised here are obtainable from all booksellers and newsagents. If you have any difficulty, please send purchase price plus 5p postage to P.O. Box 11, Falmouth, Cornwall.